Hunting Wild Turkeys in the West

by

John Higley

(All Photos By Author)

i

ISBN: 0-9628353-0-7

First Printing, Summer 1990
Second Printing, Fall 1996

Published by:
John Higley
P.O. Box 120
Palo Cedro, CA 96073

Publishing Consultant:

STONEYDALE PRESS PUBLISHING COMPANY
523 Main Street • Box 188
Stevensville, Montana 59870

Table of Contents

Introduction

Twenty years ago the prospect of hunting wild turkeys in my home state, California, wasn't even considered in my wildest daydreams. An occasional turkey hunting story appeared in national outdoor magazines, but they were all from the East, and rarely drew a second glance as I pored over the pages in search of articles on trout, mule deer, pronghorn antelope, and other things I could more readily identify with in the West.

How things change. In 1971 I was surprised with an invitation to hunt turkeys during the first spring season ever held in California, and I was urged to accept the offer by a friend in the state Department of Fish and Game, who also happened to be going along. I have never been the same since.

Since then wild turkeys have come to the West enmasse. In fact, since the 1960's they have been introduced in the states all across the country where they were never known before. From an estimated population of just 20,000 to 30,000 in 1942 the total number of turkeys across the United States has grown to more than three and a half million today. As a result, many hunters who never gave turkey hunting a second thought a few years ago are now in the fold. In the West the number of participants continues to climb with each new season.

Turkeys offer a new dimension in hunting in both spring and fall. It is a demanding sport, one that requires definite skills, and one filled with hope—and uncertainty. You never really know it all and that's why it's so interesting and fun.

What is turkey hunting like? Oddly, in the spring, the most popular time to hunt, it compares favorably with bugling for elk during the rut. Come now, you say. How can an 18 pound bird compare with a 700 pound bull elk? Well, you may not have to pack out as much meat if you're successful, but the main ingredients, challenge and sustained excitement, are still there.

To call turkeys successfully, and consistently, you have to enter the turkey's world and try to become one of them, temporarily, of course.

Some books on turkey hunting are just that–books about hunting. This book is also about hunting, but it incorporates an extra bit of background that I hope will add depth to a western hunter's understanding of his quarry. The background will not be technical in nature, but it will help when it comes down to identifying the sexes, aging gobblers, and understanding what it will take to assure wild turkey hunting for the future.

There's a certain mystery to turkey hunting, and some of the stories related between hunters certainly add to the mystique. To some, gobblers are the smartest game with two feet; to others (perish the thought) they seem fairly easy to dupe. The truth, as usual, lies somewhere in between.

If you're a newcomer, as many turkey hunters are in the West, I hope you'll learn something to help you along by reading this book. If you're an old hand I hope we'll agree on more points than not. No matter what, I hope the fun I've had hunting turkeys in the West will show through.

John Higley shows what turkey hunting in the West is all about. This fine Merriam's tom came from Montana.

To my wife, Judie,
whose patience with me
in the spring knows no bounds.

Chapter 1

Western Turkey Background

"Wild turkeys in California? You've got to be kidding." The gentleman who made that statement to me several years ago at an outdoor sports show in San Francisco was typical of many hunters throughout the West who had not yet discovered wild turkey hunting in their own states. Today many hunters still fit that mold, but many more are attracted to the sport each year like moths swirling toward a lantern at midnight.

For me, the strange fever called turkey hunting really started one evening in 1971 when four of us sat in a motel room in Paso Robles, California trying, without much success, to learn how to use box type

Thanks to trap and transplant programs western turkey hunting continues to grow. These Merriam's turkeys from South Dakota are being released in California's San Bernardino National Forest. (Jim Matthews photo)

This Rio Grande hen was trapped one evening in Northern California and transplanted by morning. (Paul Wertz photo)

Rio Grande gobblers like this fine tom are found in many western areas.
(Leonard Lee Rue III photo)

turkey calls for the first time. Some of the sounds we scraped out were as soothing as fingernails on a blackboard and the memory still makes me cringe.

It was April and the Golden State's first ever spring turkey season was going to open the next morning. Wildlife biologists Harold Harper and Chuck Graves, both active in the state Department of Fish and Game's turkey program, were confident we'd find turkeys on the ranch we were going to hunt. Of course, Chuck and Harold knew a lot about trapping and transplanting wild turkeys but we were all inexperienced when it came down to hunting techniques and turkey calling.

In the morning we split up and sallied forth with hope in our hearts and doubt in our minds. We all knew that the object was to attract a tom with hen calls, but none of us knew how much to call, or how little, how we were really supposed to sound or anything about proper calling position.

It still amazes me, but I did get my first, and the only gobbler that day, a fine 19 pound bird, but I bumped into him and five other toms while I sneaked along a ridge in the live oaks. I was excited beyond sanity when the group paraded out of a draw 35 yards away, offering me an easy shot at a tom in the open. It's no understatement to say I was both happy and proud of my prize but I was also nagged by the realization that there was something missing in my accomplishment because I didn't actually call the old fellow in. I've got to do it differently next year, I thought, as I carried my welcome load down from the hill. I realized I was hooked right then, and I still am.

New Mexico, Arizona and Colorado always had some turkeys of the Merriam's variety, but the other states west of the Rockies did not. Now, thanks to modern game management programs, hunters throughout the West are discovering what some easterners knew all along. Wild turkeys are the closest thing to big game with feathers. Unique techniques are used to hunt them, and successful hunts are the fodder for life long memories.

In the contiguous western states Nevada is the only one without turkey hunting at the moment, but despite limited habitat the Nevada Department of Wildlife successfully introduced turkeys to the Mason Valley Wildlife Area in 1987 and other areas have since been planted. Eventually, I'm sure there will at least limited wild turkey hunting in the Silver State.

Several sub-species of turkeys, all members of the family *Meleagris gallopavo*, are native to the continental U.S. They are the eastern, Florida or Osceola, Merriam's and Rio Grande. Another distinct variety is the Gould's turkey of Mexico (a small number are also present in New Mexico). Rio Grande turkeys also occur in Mexico and another member of the turkey clan, the unique ocellated turkey, is found in Central America.

Mostly in the West you'll find Rio Grande and Merriam's turkeys, though eastern turkeys have been introduced in Washington and some other states have similar plans. In their native regions Merriam's turkeys like mountainous terrain, where they adapt to a variety of associated habitat as long as there's a mixture of food producing and protective trees and shrubs, and suitable roost sites. When you think of Merriam's, think of ponderosa pines and gambel oaks, the pinyon-juniper belt, cottonwoods and willows in canyon bottoms, and wet and dry meadows where the birds feed and display.

Usually, Merriam's turkeys do not seem to be as numerous as Rio Grandes (though there are certainly exceptions in certain areas) and

The Merriam's wild turkey usually appears to be darker bodied than the Rio with whiter tail feather markings.   (Irene Vandermolen photo)

that may be because Merriam's are generally found in higher elevations where severe weather can have more affect on nesting success and over winter survival.

Ken Durbin, staff upland game biologist with the Oregon Department of Fish and Wildlife, had this to say about newly introduced Rio Grandes in his state. "Recently we had a report of a hen Rio Grande with small poults in late August.

We've never heard of anything like that with our Merriam's. It indicates that Rio Grandes are more successful than Merriam's at bringing off a brood late if their first nesting attempt fails for some reason."

Where their ranges overlap, mainly due to transplanting, Rio Grande and Merriam's turkeys interbreed freely, thus creating a hybrid that may be the most adaptable of all. In California's inland foothills most of the turkeys you see will be Rios, but in the lower mountainious regions the feather patterns vary widely, indicating cross breeding. Without getting too scientific, a general rule of thumb is that the tips

Eastern wild turkeys, which are darker than Merriam's or Rio Grandes, have been introduced in Washington and there are plans to bring them into other areas in the future.

of the rump feathers and tail feathers of a Rio Grande tom are buff colored, whereas the same feathers on a Merriam's tom are tipped with white.

The idea of bringing wild turkeys into the West (and other places where they didn't exist historically) isn't really new. Even while native turkey populations in the East were being threatened with extinction, due to habitat destruction and unregulated hunting, California's early Fish and Game Commission obtained wild turkeys from Mexico and released them in the San Bernardino Mountains in the southern part of the state. That release failed, but it was made in 1908!

Colorado started trying to improve the situation for the native Merriam's there in the early 1940s. California was seriously engaged in the turkey business from 1928 through 1951. During that time 3,350 turkeys were raised on game farms and released in 71 different places.

Only three attempts were mildly successful and the program was eventually dropped. Some people suggested that wild turkeys would never be important in California. Funny, you don't hear talk like that these days.

What happened in my home state during the 1960s was happening throughout the country during the same period of time. The introduction of new trapping methods, including rocket propelled cannon nets, allowed the capture of dozens of turkeys at one time, whereby the birds were transferred quickly to predetermined release sites.

The system worked so well that one biologist in California said, "When we released some Rio Grandes from Texas into some of our blue oak foothill country they didn't know they ever left home."

Most western states got their first birds from trapping operations elsewhere, often through reciprocal trades for other species of game. That kind of cooperation is still in effect but now more and more states are enlarging their turkey range with transplants of their own resident wild birds. All in all it's a success story game departments, and the sportsmen who back them, can be justifiably proud of.

Chapter 2

The Western Difference

Although it may be argued, with some accuracy, that turkey hunting is turkey hunting no matter where you are, and that techniques that work in one place can work in another, there are some differences in hunting turkeys "out West" just as there are variations in the way people live in different geographical areas.

Aside from population centers, the West is still much more open than the East and terrain variations are more notable. They affect the way hunters hunt and the way turkeys live. In my home state of California, for instance, it is not impossible to start a turkey hunt a few hundred feet above sea level in rolling foothills and end it at 4,000 feet elevation a few hours later, after driving less than an hour between locations. Sometimes a hunter who tries high ground at daybreak will find himself in rain or blizzard conditions, while valley areas are calm and even sunny.

Western turkeys occupy an amazing range of habitat. I've hunted birds in canyon country so rugged that the turkeys could not walk along the bottom and had to fly to get around. And I've spotted them sharing the same opening with mule deer on a high plateau at 7,000 feet elevation where there was also a population of elk. It is common in the West for Merriam's turkeys, and Rio Grandes in some areas, to migrate to the valleys for the winter then climb to higher elevations as the breeding season approaches.

Weather is definitely a limiting factor in such varied terrain, especially at higher elevations. Wes Keyes, Information Management Supervisor for the Arizona Game and Fish Department, noted that access roads into Arizona turkey habitat can be terrible in the spring, and a real detriment to hunter success. I've encountered similar conditions in Wyoming, Oregon and Montana but they didn't stop the guys I was with, or me, from hunting those places successfully, although foul weather did chase me out of New Mexico one year.

It was in the northeastern part of the state where Mike Ballew, of

Raton, and I hunted the edge of a giant mesa for Merriam's turkeys at 7,000 feet elevation. It was ranch country, quite open in the bottom-lands, with large cottonwood trees along the streams, ribbons of ponderosa pines accentuating the slopes, and juniper thickets outlining sagebrush openings and grassy meadows.

It was big country and sometimes the turkeys were so far away that we couldn't hear the toms gobble, but we found them with binoculars first, then got into position for calling, and it worked beautifully. We got three toms in two days time (the limit was two per season in the region) but then a genuine blizzard hit and even closed the paved highways for a couple days. By the time conditions improved I was already back home in California.

I can also vouch for the fact that even in sunny California 4-wheel drive sometimes isn't quite enough. In the Golden State, for instance,

Some western hunting areas are vast and open. Here John Higley carries a Rio Grande tom out of the pine dotted mountains of southern Oregon.

my friend Phil Grunert often hunted turkeys successfully in mountainous terrain between the North Coast and the northern Sacramento
Valley when few others were aware the birds were there. It was an
enviable situation but Phil normally had to wait for the snow to melt
several weeks into the five week season, and then he had to hike for
hours to reach the birds. Judging from his sly grin whenever he was
asked if he got anything—he usually did.

One key to Phil's success was timing, an important consideration in
any part of the West. In higher elevations and northern latitudes the

*Some of the open terrain in the West looks like this mixture of pine and oak
at 4,000 feet elevation.*

best spring hunting of all may occur during the last third of the season,
both from the standpoint of improving weather and road conditions, and
increased breeding activity on the part of the turkeys. In northern
California, though, by far the best hunting in 1990 took place during the
first two weeks of the season after which unusually warm, dry weather
conditions seemed to put a damper on gobbling activity.

In Montana, wildlife biologist Rob Hazlewood, an avid turkey hunter
who also manufactures Cedar Hill elk and turkey calls, notes that
western turkeys respond actively to weather conditions of the moment.

On a nice spring day they'll gobble up a storm but a passing weather front may make them clam up completely. Rob's advice is simply to be flexible enough to take advantage of the prime periods, and he's right.

On the other hand, more than once I was glad I went out, despite pouring rain that greeted me when the alarm went off at 3 o'clock in the morning, because the storm broke by daybreak and soon after the sun came out the toms dried off and started gobbling as if nothing happened.

It is widely believed by experienced hunters from the East that western turkeys are actually more vocal and easier to call than their eastern counterparts. Considering the extra heavy hunting pressure in some states east of the Mississippi that would not surprise me in the least. However, our so-called easy toms can be frustrating as the devil at times, and there are some places, especially in California, where there are more than enough hunters to keep the birds on their toes.

After hearing about Alabama's tight-lipped toms I finally hunted there in 1990 and found the rumors about toms that don't gobble much to be basically true. However, there are definitly exceptions. I killed one tom in a heavily hunted area that gobbled several times before flying down from the roost practically into my lap. Later I visited private land where the birds gobbled as much as any I've ever encountered in the West. The incidence of silent toms seems to be more a matter of concentrated hunting pressure, the availability of hens, competition among gobblers, and long term weather conditions than geographical location.

Even if the turkeys do respond better to calling in parts of the West, finding them in the first place is a challenge of unparalleled difficulty between East and West simply because the amount of habitat out here is so vast, and not all of it has birds by any means.

"In the West you might be looking at 100 square miles of mountains at a time," Rob Hazlewood said. "Sure you've been told there are turkeys in the range, but where do you start? In most places you simply don't have the turkey population density of the southeast so out here homework is a major part of turkey hunting long before you ever get out in the field."

In most of the 11 western states represented here turkey numbers are stable or increasing. Hunter interest is also climbing every year throughout the region and I can vouch personally for the excellent opportunities available in New Mexico, Montana, Oregon, Idaho, Wyoming and my home state California.

Spring hunting regulations in the West are similar to those found

Turkeys range from the mountains to the river bottoms in the West. This canyon habitat is below the 1,000 foot mark in northern California.

nationwide and seasons vary in length from two to five weeks. Most states also allow fall hunting and in a few the use of rifles is permitted spring and fall. True, rifle turkey hunting is permitted in a few states east of the Rockies, but I've never seen it practiced anywhere but in the West. In fact, the first wild turkey I ever saw up close was killed by a rifle hunter in New Mexico's Gila Wilderness many moons ago.

One reason such hunting is allowed is that big game and wild turkey seasons sometimes overlap and it's not unusual for deer hunters, for instance, to come across bands of turkeys occasionally. Rifle turkey hunting was actually the norm during deer seasons in places like New Mexico before spring hunting really took hold in the West and some hunters still do not realize there's any better way. I do not intend to voice criticism about a legal activity, and if a hunter is skillful enough to bag a wild turkey with his pet rifle without destroying the meat, more power to him. However, when it comes down to turkey hunting on its own merit the heart of the sport lays in close range encounters with these wary birds and the skills necessary to call the them into shotgun or bow range, spring or fall, are what this book is all about.

I realize there's a centuries long tradition behind turkey hunting in the East and the best hunters from that region can teach all of us who reside in the West something about the nuances of the sport if we will only listen. Western hunters are obviously much newer at the game and for the most part the competition between hunters here is not as great. But you know, from talking with turkey hunters from Montana to Oregon, and points in between, that turkey hunters in the West are on a straight path to a tradition of their own. Wild turkeys, it seems, are here to stay.

As we continue, the things described herein will apply to hunting turkeys in the West according to the conditions I've encountered in several different states, and the information other turkey hunting fanatics have volunteered with only minimum arm twisting on my part. I wish I knew it all, and never made mistakes, but I don't and I do. But then, if turkeys were always predictable anyone could figure them out and hunting them wouldn't be nearly as much fun as it is.

Chapter 3

Knowing The Bird

It's my impression that quite a few turkey hunters view their sport superficially—that is, without in-depth understanding of the birds they're after. That is no crime, of course, but the more you learn about turkeys, the more interesting this already fascinating sport becomes.

Calling is usually emphasized in seminars and videos, and there's nothing wrong with that, but you really need to know more to get to the heart of what can be a most involving, and fascinating pastime. That's my impression anyway, and perhaps the following ancedote will bear me out.

It took place on a clear April morning in northern California when the sun's early rays illuminated the hilltops but before they reached the valley floor. A half hour earlier Jim Dorsey and I heard more than one distant gobbler sound off after leaving their roosts. It took awhile for us to get to the spot, however, and by then the toms were quiet as mice in the chicken feed. Realizing that they were probably close, even though we didn't hear them, we tucked in behind an old barbed wire fence and a screen of brush next to a gnarled oak, whereby I made a few yelps with my favorite box call. Even before the echo died a single haunting gobble broke the stillness.

I called a few more times at intervals of a few minutes but I didn't hear anything until an odd, almost inaudible sound, turned my head like a "clink" in the night. "Phfft, baroooom, phfft, baroooom!"

"Hear that, Jim?" I hissed. "There's a gobbler coming down the hill!"

I shifted my gaze toward the brush line just across the grassy opening before us, and watched intently for any sign of movement. I wasn't sure that my partner, who was new to turkey hunting, believed I was serious, but I sure hoped he did. The tom may not have been gobbling, but I could hear him strutting up a storm.

A few more soft hen yelps were all it took to lure the tom into view and Jim bagged him with a single round of well placed No.4 shot. Later, while we admired his prize, I asked Jim if he heard anything at all

A strutting tom is a pretty picture to a hen turkey from the caruncle beads on his forehead and neck to his extended snood–seen here draping over his beak.

before the tom stepped into sight.

"I thought I heard a car start far away," he replied, "It was hollow, like it was in a tunnel."

Actually, Jim's description was good. A tom's drumming sound, or pulmonic puff if you want to get technical, really can be mistaken for something else except for the fact that it usually happens over and over. The tom's wings flex slightly when the energetic, internal "phfft!" sound is made and then his fanned tail feathers vibrate enough to hum. No one knows exactly why a tom does this but apparently it really impresses the ladies and often it's the only noise they make while strutting.

On the other hand the drumming often occurs between his excited gobbles and sometimes when a tom is coming your way, and gobbling

15

only sporadically, the sound of his drumming will let you know that he's getting close—if you're aware of what the sound is and can hear it. Luckily, recognizing that subdued noise, while helpful, is not always critical to bagging a turkey because it depends not only on one's ability to really concentrate but on keen hearing, which not all of us have. Being aware of as much as possible is an integral part of turkey hunting, however, and can make the difference between success and another tale about the one that got away.

Adult toms have beautiful round tails like this.

When I first started hunting turkeys I knew what the birds looked like, that the toms strutted and the hens didn't, and that they were awfully good to eat, especially on Thanksgiving. That was about the extent of my understanding. But turkey hunting is such a consuming sport that most really involved hunters simply can't hunt the birds very often and not try to figure out what makes them tick.

I don't remember when I first realized that strutting males did anything more than dance around and gobble, but I do know that learning to listen for things like the "puff" has, without question, made me a better hunter.

16

Obviously, the first thing newcomers to turkey hunting need to know is how to distinguish between toms and hens, especially during the spring when only males are legal game. To begin with the hens are a little lighter in appearance. Their grayish-blue heads have a sprinkling of tiny feathers, and their body feathers have buff colored tips. All in all their coloration provides good camouflage for the hens while they're incubating eggs. Mature hens are also smaller than mature males.

The tail of a one year old tom (a jake) will have longer central feathers like this.

Toms stand taller than hens and they appear almost black from a distance except for their wings and tail. Their body feathers are dark and tipped with black but they do glow with shades of bronze in sunlight.

Better clues are the gobbler's bald head and neck, which are much more colorful than those of hens. The presence of a beard in the middle of the breast is normally a sure sign to go by, though a small percentage of hens do grow them, too.

A gobbler's head and neck parts have particular names and many hunters can't identify them. Perhaps this run down will help. Caruncle refers to the wart-like projections on the skin at the upper part of the forehead and to the bead-like whattling from under the bird's chin to the feather line on the neck. The loose flap of skin sometimes apparent beneath the chin is the dewlap. And the retractable pencil-like projection on top of a tom's head, just above the beak, is the snood or leader.

The head and neck have a multitude of colors ranging from bluish-white, to red, to blue with a hint of purple. The colors change rapidly to fit a gobbler's mood of the moment. While strutting, or otherwise performing for hens, the skull cap appears almost white but the whattles usually enlarge with blood and turn vivid red. However, a gobbler's head and neck can also be almost whitish as he struts and displays. I suspect, but can't prove, that this posture is used quite often when a tom thinks there's a hen in the vicinity but hasn't seen her as yet. Etched against a background of flared, dark tail feathers his head and neck are almost as striking as a candle in the dark.

The snood, which is retracted when the tom is not aroused, expands and droops across his beak as part of the breeding display.

From the western hunter's standpoint a hen is usually just a hen,

The bristle-like beards worn by toms are actually primitive feathers called mesofiloplumnes.

but males go by several names such as tom, gobbler, boss tom (or boss gobbler), and jake. Just to confuse matters, the term "boss" refers to a dominant male in a particular area, or situation. He may be alone or traveling with several other adult or young males. In any event he will have established authority over the others through bluffs and actual fighting and he will attract most of the available hens. Generally, the "boss" of a group is the tom that gobbles first, and struts the most, and does the breeding. Nothing is cut and dried in the world of turkeys, however, and many a young tom (jake) has filled the role of boss where bigger, older birds are absent for one reason or another.

Incidentally, you can recognize a strutting adult or jake from a distance by observing the tail feathers. Adult toms, two years old and older, have evenly rounded tail feathers, as seen when the tail is fanned. Jakes are males hatched the previous spring and they have longer central tail feathers and thus an uneven fan until the second moult.

One question often asked of successful turkey hunters is, "How long was his beard?" That's because a long beard identifies an adult that has made it through more than one hunting season. Some hunters feel a tom like that has acquired an extra degree of wariness, and while that

The tom that wore this spur, which was 7/8 of an inch long, was probably about 3 years old.

19

may be true to some extent if the bird has been hunted recently, I doubt if any adult tom is immune to calling totally, especially if he isn't with hens on a particular spring day. The trick, as usual, is to put yourself in the right place at the right time, and to do the right thing under the circumstances. Regardless, bagging an old long bearded gobbler is an accomplishment dedicated turkey hunters relish and strive for.

In case you're curious, a tom's beard, which looks like a slim, long bristle brush emanating from the center of the breast, is actually a group of primitive feathers known as mesofiloplumnes. The total beard may have anywhere from a few dozen to hundreds of individual strands. Incidentally, when a rare hen does grow a beard it is usually thinner and shorter than those of males.

Toms in the same age class may have beards of different lengths and

These primary wing feathers from an adult tom show wear from strutting.

thickness. The bristles continue to grow throughout a tom's life, but wear and breakage limit the overall length. Adult gobblers commonly have 8 or 9 inch beards and some grow them 11 or 12 inches long. Rarely, a tom will sport a 13 inch adornment—or longer. The longest beard I've heard of in my part of the country belonged to a tom bagged by Californian Al Tisserand in Shasta County during the spring season in 1985. I measured it at 14 and 7/8s inches and it was probably that long because the tom had injured a leg at one time and couldn't bend over normally. Thus, the beard didn't drag as much as usual.

On jakes the beards may be quite short and hard to spot protruding

Hens, like this one sitting on her nest in California, are the key to perpetuating any turkey flock. That's why only gobblers are hunted in the spring.

through the breast feathers, though some are several inches long. Additionally, there are common instances where toms grow multiple beards of varying lengths. One such adult that I saw a few years ago had four separate beards and a jake I killed in 1985 had three, the longest of which was only 3-1/2 inches.

Although beards are obviously longer on adult toms than they are on jakes they are poor signs by which to estimate age because there are so many variables involved. A better gauge are the spurs that usually develop on a tom turkey's legs. They are a fairly accurate indication of age—up to a point.

On jakes the spurs are just buttons that don't protrude from the back of their legs. By the second year they may be a half inch long and a three year old male may have spurs an inch in length, pointed but not sharp. In older gobblers the spurs are usually curved slightly upward and sharp on the ends, but rarely do they exceed an inch and a half in length. As usual, however, nothing is set in concrete with turkeys. The growth rate of the spurs may vary somewhat with the individual and they seem to stop growing altogether by the time a tom is a four year old senior citizen.

One other indicator of age is the outer primary wing feathers, which are barred to the tip in adults and rounded somewhat (although strutting will wear them off because they drag on the ground). On immature turkeys the tips are usually sharp and the barring does not extend all the way down through the last inch or so.

Gobblers lead tough lives, as a golden eagle killed carcass proved to me once again in west/central Idaho a few years back. The tom was a nice Merriam's with a 9 inch beard, which I found, but he was no match for the winged predator. There were turkey feathers scattered for 50 yards along an old skid trail but the eagle finally won the tussle. Actually, most turkeys succumb to predation, illness or weather related problems a few days after they hatch, but the same can be said of other upland game such as pheasants, grouse and quail.

Hunting obviously has something to do with their mortality as adults but it's a rare predator that will not dine on turkey when the opportunity arises. In fact, most grown turkeys only live a couple of years so the older adults have already beat the odds. As for hens, they are usually fair game for hunting in the fall but they are not pursued actively during springtime when they, too, would be more vulnerable. One of the oldest wild turkeys on record was a bearded hen that was mistaken for a tom and killed during the spring in northern California. She was apparently 11 years old, as was proven by a band she wore since being released by the department of fish and game years before. She was definitly the exception to the rule.

Naturally, hunters are more interested in toms than hens, especially in the spring when gobblers alone are facing the gun. However, the hens are the key to perpetuating the flock and the future supply of toms. They lay their clutch of eggs over a period of several days in ground nests (really a simple depression in a sheltered spot). After the clutch (usually 8 to 12 but sometimes more speckled, buff-white eggs) is laid the hen will start to incubate the eggs and she'll stick it out through all sorts of weather for 28 days. While the hens will get up once in awhile for a drink or to peck around a little, I once kept tabs on an experienced adult while she sat for 15 days straight in blistering heat, thus keeping her eggs at the right temperature until the weather moderated a bit.

It's interesting to note, incidentally, that a hen remains fertile for several weeks after breeding, giving her time to lay a second clutch should her first clutch be destroyed somehow or should she be forced to abandon it for some reason.

A hen's work isn't over just because her brood hatches, either. While the poults are small she must protect them from the heat, cold and moisture with her body, show them what and where to eat and drink, and constantly be on the lookout for predators on the ground and in the air. On the ground or on a tree roost a hen will extend her wings over her poults to protect them from weather and predators. It's when the poults are a little too big to shelter yet not fully feathered that they most often succumb to such natural calamities as sudden spring downpours and hailstorms.

Despite a hen's best efforts, predators and disasters often take a significant percentage of her brood. But, bobcats, coyotes, hawks, eagles and owls aside, wild turkeys are resilient enough to face natural predation, occasional poor nesting conditions and sport hunting and not only survive but maintain or increase in population from year to year. The success of even small plants of wild birds throughout the West is ample proof of that.

All game birds have interesting individual characteristics, of course, but no others are legally hunted during the spring breeding season. A turkey hunter, then, by virtue of the very hunting techniques he uses, is submerged, at least to his neck, in a turkey's unique brand of life. That's why observing turkeys, and trying to understand why they do what they do, is so important.

Chapter 4

Calls And Calling

"Boy, you should have been there," the guy leaning across the counter of the local sporting goods store said. *"I clucked twice, yelped four times three minutes later, clucked again, and before I knew it that old tom was right in my lap!"*

Such talk is common during the spring season when turkey hunting occupies the mind of any man stuck on the great birds, but everytime I hear an exact rundown of the calls used to fool the smartest old gobbler in the woods (they all are, you know) I wonder if

Here are only a few of the many types of turkey calls available to hunters. This assortment includes both friction and air operated calls.

the fellow carries a tape recorder in his pocket to record each call made. Personally, I find it difficult to remember just what I did to lure in a tom only minutes before, and impossible to predict what I'll do next time around. I get involved in each encounter and do what seems right for the moment.

The truth of the matter is that while the importance of calling cannot be overstated there are no absolutes in turkey hunting. While some guys call very little, some call a lot and tom turkeys respond to each on occasion, and neither at other times.

Another thing to remember is that the same calling devices will sound differently when used by different hunters, as will different types of calls used by the same hunter. While it helps to be proficient with more than one type of call, and to be able to make a variety of turkey sounds with some idea of what they mean, you do not have to be a calling contest winner to bag turkeys regularly. Frankly, some of the worst calling I've ever heard has been made by genuine turkey hens.

Calling is the primary method of turkey hunting in the spring no matter where you are. When the gobblers are actively seeking hens for breeding putting yourself in a hen's place is the necessary ingre-

This hunter is using a box call, one of the most reliable and easy to operate turkey calls of all.

dient for consistent success. In the fall calling is also important, but sometimes to a lesser degree.

Taken as a group there is almost as much variety in turkey calls alone as there is in duck, goose, elk and predator calls combined. It's a confusing array to choose from, but it's not as difficult as it seems. Bear in mind that any type of call can work so it all boils down mostly to personal preference—which call(s) suit you best. Part of the fun, of course, is in trying different types of calls when the mood moves you so many turkey hunters have two or three types with them whenever they hunt.

To simplify a complex subject let's classify turkey calls two ways— as friction and air operated. The hard part lays in separating the various types of calls in each category without making things too complex in the process. But enough preliminary. Let's take a look at friction calls which have probably been popular in one form or another since the first turkey hunter looked that first old gobbler in the eye.

The largest group of friction calls are the box calls which come in many sizes and tones. Basically, they are all hollow, rectangular, hand held boxes, mostly made of cedar or mahogany (other woods and even plastic are in use now), that have swinging lids (or paddles) attached with a screw in front. When the paddle is scraped across the lip, or lips of the box at the right angle amazingly accurate turkey calls result. Today there are even push button box calls that are almost fool proof and great for beginners.

With any box you can reproduce several types of turkey talk including clucks, yelps, purrs, cutts, the cackle and on some boxes, even gobbles.

It's generally agreed that a typical box call is about the easiest call for a beginner to learn on. In fact, no matter how long you hunt turkeys a quality box call will continue to call toms for you as long as you keep it chalked properly (every call comes with directions), dry, and don't sit on it like I did one of mine. Actually, I glued that cracked box back together and it's still a favorite.

One problem with a standard box call is that the lid can move at the wrong time and make noise while you're walking unless you put rubber bands around it or carry it in a specially made holster. With a scratch box, a box with a detached striker, this trouble is eliminated and some hunters prefer them for that reason. Also, they're less cumbersome and fit easily into a pocket. Personally, I still like a regular cedar box because the sounds I make with them seem better

26

A nice Merriam's tom and the calls that did him in–a box and diaphragm calls. Note the binoculars which are often handy in the West.

to me. That, too, is personal preference at work but I feel the tones from a box call can occasionally elicit a response from a tom that would ignore another type of call.

Take a thin piece of slate, glue it to a round or rectangular wood or plastic holder and you have a basic slate call. These calls are

27

operated with wood or plastic strikers, which, when scraped across the slate in the proper manner, emit about the same array of calls as a box. They are somewhat different in tone, however, and some hunters use their slates more than anything else. Among other things they make the prettiest soft yelps, clucks and purrs you ever heard as well as the raspy "cutting" used to excite a gobbler or challenge the hens he's with so they'll lead him to you.

Cup a slate in your hand, or against your belly or leg, and the smooth resonance you hear will tell you why such calls are so popular. They sound inviting, but for me they are not as easy to use as box calls, and the sound does not seem to carry as far, which can be an advantage or disadvantage, depending on circumstances.

There are also friction calls that incorporate a thin strip of aluminum or slate in the middle of a resonant holder, such as the Sweet Talker from Penn's Woods and Ben Lee's Super Hen (modeled after the Raymond Chrisholm call) and these do make seductive tones when the strikers are properly applied.

Many years ago, my grandfather, who was from Pennsylvania originally, showed me how to hollow out a turkey wing bone one Thanksgiving and make a turkey call out of it. At the time I was in grammar school in Los Angeles, and had no idea what a real turkey sounded like, but I took his word for it and spent part of the day sucking on the wing bone much like a straw.

It's funny how things stick with you. Even today I make a wing bone call for fun occasionally, and while I've never used one in the field, I know the sounds I make sucking air through it would certainly work if the right turkey came along.

The wing bone was, in effect, my first air operated turkey call. An improvement over actual bone models are the tube yelpers now made of plastic and wood, which look better and are quite easy to use with a little practice. Suck air properly through a tube yelper and you can make sounds that carry across canyons.

Besides the thin tube yelpers, there are short, round tube calls that resemble pill bottles or plastic film containers. They have a latex diaphragm stretched across one end, and require that you huff air through them rather than drawing it in.

There are also horseshoe shaped diaphragm calls which fit entirely inside the mouth, and are operated by puffs of air from your throat. Diaphragms are the most difficult calls to master because they will make some people gag and won't fit in everyone's mouth correctly, especially if you wear a dental plate. Still, these are very popular calls because you can use them without any hand movement at all. Diaphragms come with anywhere from one to four reeds and each has a different tone. I use a double reed type most of the time and I sometimes cheat just a little and cut three or four very tiny slits in the edge of the reed(s) with a razor blade, making the call sound raspier than usual. Any sound a turkey makes can be reproduced adequately with a diaphragm, though I personally shy away from trying to gobble with them.

Instead, I carry a gobble tube, a call that produces a gobble when you shake it. There's more than one type of gobble tube on the market these days, and as I said earlier there are some box calls that you can gobble with, as well.

There are other types of calls to be sure, and new ones appear on the market practically every year. In the end the type of call you rely on most is strictly a matter of personal preference. Most of the experienced turkey hunters I know eventually acquire several different kinds and carry more than one with them while hunting. It makes things more interesting, and there are definitely times when one tone seems to appeal to a gobbler more than another. For my own hunting I rely on a box call and diaphragms about equally. Tucked away in my daypack is a slate, and sometimes a gobble tube, and usually a noise maker call (I'll review noise makers shortly) as well.

First, there's one more call to point out—namely the human voice. Some hunters can get by on vocal chords alone. For instance, my friend Eldon Bergman, who's been guiding turkey hunters in California since the first spring season was held there, rarely uses a manufactured call. The yelps, clucks, and gobbles that come from his throat are convincing enough for most any turkey in the woods. That just proves that turkeys will respond to any type of call as long as it sounds somewhat realistic.

According to one source, turkeys make eight basic calls but there are variations of them all depending, among other things, on the age and sex of individual birds. Another study categorizes nearly 30 sounds, which is far more than most of us will ever need to know. Their basic vocabulary, stated simply, includes the yelp, cluck, cackle, purr, alarm putt, the kee-kee whistle of young birds, the kee-kee run and the gobble.

Another sound that is being used more and more by turkey hunters is cutting, which was mentioned previously in this chapter. Cutting is a burst of sharp clucks, with occasional coarse purrs mixed in. I've heard cutting when two hens were threatening one another

A hunter tries to locate a tom with his slate call somewhere in the Oregon woods. Slate calls are the favorites of many hunters.

for one reason or another. Whatever it means to a turkey, cutting excites some gobblers so it is a useful addition to your selection of calls. Though cutting, like everything else in turkey hunting, can be overdone when used too much.

The hen yelp is the hunter's real workhorse call. If that's the only turkey sound you can make you'll call turkeys eventually, once you learn the hunting techniques. The yelp means everything from "Here I am." "To where are you?" It can be used loud to locate a tom and start him on his way in, or softly to make him think a hen is about to fly out of her tree at daybreak, or that she's wandering off, or just being coy behind that bush where you're sitting.

Prospective turkey hunters sometimes worry too much about how many yelps to use in a series. Sometimes four or five yelps do the job; other times you might make a dozen. Some real hens carry on more than you ever will; some hardly talk at all. Just remember a few slow, throaty yelps are usually made by a tom. Hen yelps are a bit faster and higher pitched, though they may also be soft, loud or raspy depending on the circumstances.

As far as I'm concerned the cluck is about equal to the yelp as a useful call. Used discreetly it works wonders on reluctant, heavily hunted birds. You've got to be prudent, but I like to cluck now and then between yelps as a sort of "Here I am" convincer. Turkeys often cluck-purr softly as they feed contentedly and your ability to make such a sound might, just might, help convince a reluctant old tom that you're the real thing some day. I almost always get very quiet when I know a tom is committed and just cluck lightly, or purr a little, to let him know I'm still close-by or to make him think the hen of his dreams is actually walking slowly away.

The alarm putt has already been mentioned but it warrants more attention. Often the first thing a turkey does when it's scared or suspicious of something is "putt" sharply a number of times as it walks stiffly away or just before it breaks into a run or flies. Another turkey that hears the outburst may or may not leave just as quickly, but you can almost bet that when an old hen "putts" nervously that any gobbler nearby will suddenly get lockjaw and head for greener pastures. Some hunters worry that their clucks will sound something like alarm putts to a turkey but that will rarely, if ever, happen if you limit your clucks to one or two and do not interject a sense of urgency by clucking sharply a number of times. You can almost imagine a turkey saying, "I'm over here," when it clucks and a Monty Python like "run away, run away," when it putts. Really.

John Higley with a Merriam's turkey from Idaho. This tom was fooled by a few yelps from a diaphragm call but any one of several types of calls probably would have done the job.

The kee-kee whistle is made by young birds through the summer and fall while they're still with their mother hens. The kee-kee often precedes a series of yelps to form the kee-kee run. This call is used mostly in the fall by hunters trying to call young birds in after scattering a flock for just that purpose. However, the kee-kee sound does prompt some gobblers to respond in the spring so it can be useful for locating them at times.

A sudden series of "cuts" usually made by a hen just leaving the roost, is known as the cackle. Most hunters have never heard it in the woods but the cackle will add to your arsenal of calls and it can be effective at certain times. However, the cackle normally denotes the movement of a turkey flying up, down or across and it might tell a gobbler that the hen of his dreams is either leaving the area or coming to him and that could cost you a chance. On the other hand, you might cackle at daybreak to indicate that a hen has just left her roost, and that might start a tom coming to that location. For awhile the cackle was touted as something of a wonder call. In realty, it's a substitute call to use sparingly when a simple yelp doesn't seem like enough.

I'm not too sure that the cackle, used during the course of a long conversation with any one of several old toms I can think of, was the convincer that finally lured him in. When you relate the cackle to movement you can readily see why. Actually, you're more apt to lure a tom with excited, rapid yelps or clucks than the cackle.

Of course, the sound that sets every hunter on edge with anticipation is the unbridled gobble of a lusty tom trying to attract, or coming to a hen. The gobble tells a hen(s) where Mr. Turkey is and is the most vocal part of a tom's breeding efforts.

A little gobbling goes a very long way when it comes to hunter use, though. For one thing a gobble at the wrong time, by you, might scare a real tom halfway out of the county unless he's in the mood for a challenge. Basically, unless you use a gobble to make a tom sound off in the early morning just before sunrise, so you'll know where he is, the gobble is one call to use sparingly at most. The usual idea is to present a challenge to another tom in his territory and make him mad enough to come looking for the interloper. Once in a great while it does just that, and sometimes, if you happen to gobble at subordinate birds, you might simply chase them away.

I used the gobble for better or worse under unusual circumstances one morning in 1985 with surprising results. A few days earlier I tried to converse like a friendly hen with a pair of toms roosted a couple of hundred yards apart along the same drainage. But while they both answered my hen yelps from their trees they seemed interested only in each other when they finally flew down. I could hear their gobbles getting closer together and when they met they both shut up with the suddenness of a door closing. It was very late in the hunting season and I figured that the toms were merely looking for company and weren't interested in the opposite sex. The hens, I thought, were probably nesting somewhere and the toms in that particular spot had been badgered by hunters for weeks.

Two days later I was back, armed with a different game plan, one I'd never used before anyway. In the dark I found a convenient place to sit against a large black oak tree with the branches of a large manzanita bush directly overhead and off to one side. It was a cozy spot, appreciated all the more when sooty clouds playing wind tag in the dark sky started spitting rain.

I didn't touch a call until hearing the first gobble of the day, telling me that at least one of the toms was still around. Then, instead of yelping back, I shook my gobble tube like mad as if to say, "Over here, buddy. Let's go out for breakfast together."

A few minutes later I saw movement across the meadow that separated me from the roost tree. Surprisingly, it was a hen trotting my way with determination. I switched to the throaty yelps of a gobbler, really raspy and deep, and she came on steadily. Meanwhile, the tom was still gobbling somewhere in the brush line along the right side of the opening. This was getting interesting, indeed.

Shortly, the hen was just 15 feet away, staring at my hiding place, expecting to see another turkey. When she didn't, she got nervous and started putting (don't keep that up, I prayed) as she walked off to my right through an opening.

I knew it was all over. She'll join the tom soon and they'll take a hike, I thought, but I started more coarse yelping and clucking anyway. A minute later the hen was back and this time the gobbler was right behind her. It was a jake Rio Grande and I don't think she wanted anything to do with him. I did, though, and I shot him at 15 yards. The clouds were passing, the air was sweet with the smell of rain, and I was delighted, to say the least. I still have the nagging feeling that somewhere in the area there was a boss tom and that the hen thought I was him.

Finally, it should be noted that gobbling isn't a good idea in heavily hunted areas for reasons I'll explain later. I knew I had that private land to myself or I wouldn't have started the day off the way I did.

Now, how does a newcomer learn the actual sounds he should know? It shouldn't be too difficult, really. If you live in an area where turkey hunting is growing in popularity chances are good that the local sporting goods store has a line of calls as well as instruction records and tapes that cover everything you need to know to get started. Videos are also popular. Later there will be a list of call manufacturers that you can contact for details on their lines.

Chapter 5

Noise Makers

As if the array of calls just described in chapter four isn't enough there are also the noise makers—or locator calls—that are used by turkey hunters but which may not be turkey calls at all. Noise makers are used specifically to get a response from a gobbler, to make him sound off instinctively and give his location away. That will let you know where he's roosting before he would normally start gobbling at daybreak, or help you find a tom sometime during the day without alerting him to the presence of a bogus hen (you), and when gobbling in general is at a minimum.

Like anything else the noise makers don't work all of the time, and I think there are cases when they are used too much by hunters and

These calls can be classified as noise makers. They include an owl hooter, two types of crow calls and a gobble tube.

gradually lose their desired effect. On the other hand, noise makers are worth a try in a pinch.

Before dawn in the spring, for instance, you might be able to locate a gobbler on the roost by hooting like an owl with your voice or a call. In the West most hunters try to sound like a great horned owl simply because the sound is one turkeys hear naturally. East of the Rockies hunters usually try to duplicate a barred owl, instead. Actually, the barred owl call would work in the West, too, and probably better than the softer notes of the great horned owl. Of course, most of the time the only answer you'll get is from a genuine owl somewhere in the dark. Interestingly, some western hunters have learned to yap like our ever present coyotes with a diaphragm call and those sounds will also wake a tom up occasionally before daylight.

But what is the advantage to you of screaming in the woods like a banshee even if a tom does answer? Well, sometimes a single response in the dark will lead you to a better spot to call from at daybreak. I regularly hunt an area with four commonly used roosts spread out over a square mile or so. Just a single gobble early tells me exactly where those birds are on that particular morning.

In any event, the idea is to make a sudden noise and shock a tom into gobbling back. Sometimes, just sometimes, turkeys will answer practically any noise including fake gobbles, predator calls, sonic booms, car horns, etc.

One of the most amusing and interesting spring mornings I ever had in the turkey woods was with fellow outdoor writer Dwight Schuh and our mutual friend Cliff Dewell in northern California. The occasion was Dwight's first turkey hunt and to set the scene we were about to get lucky. Three toms had just gobbled back at Cliff's yelps from high on a ridge and we were hiking as fast as we could to close the gap and start calling seriously.

When we figured we were no more than 100 yards from the birds Dwight sat down against a stump and Cliff and I moved back a few yards to call. The plan was to sound like more than one hen without going overboard, but we needn't have worried because we soon had unexpected company when a helicopter started circling directly overhead. I have never heard more excited gobbling than when we called while the chopper blades whirred above the ridge. Whap, whap,whap,whap. "Gobble-obble-obble-gobbleobbleobblegobbleobble-obble!"

It was pure bedlam and it still makes me smile when I think of the three jakes that went crazy when a copter helped us talk turkey.

Ed Sweet uses a crow call to locate turkeys in western Idaho.

Yes, Dwight did get his first tom right there.

As we've seen, sometimes shaking a gobble tube will make a tom open up as the first hint of dawn appears on the horizon, and it may do the same thing later in the day. Rather than taking the risk of intimidating a tom by gobbling, though, you might get him to answer a crow call if it's shrill enough even if there are real crows in the vicinity.

One incredible hunt a few years ago in the northern California foothills sold me on using a crow call periodically on certain days. At the time I was guiding a hunter on heavily hunted property where there were turkeys, certainly, but where actually calling one of the spooky toms in was getting tougher all the time because of the pressure.

We heard a pair of toms on their roosts just at daybreak. They gobbled three or four times each, then flew down and gobbled a couple of times on the ground. I yelped a few times with a diaphragm and they gobbled back for a minute or two but moved steadily away. Perhaps they knew a real hen could catch up easily. Finally, they clammed up completely and I figured a hen had, indeed, joined them.

The hunter could walk pretty well so we quickly circled the birds' last known position and tried calling again. The silence was deafening, and I, for one, thought the trend for the morning was set. Badgered toms like those two survivors can be almost impossible to call in. I wondered if they were even in the vicinity anymore and decided to blow a crow call in hopes of finding out. I reached into my shirt pocket, got mine out, and blew six or seven sharp blasts across the hills.

"Gobble-obble-obble!" One distant gobble. It wasn't much but we knew the turkeys were on the hilltop above us. We hurried up the slope, thankful the sun wasn't high and warm yet, and stopped before reaching the crest. I yelped softly a few times and heard nothing.

We crossed the ridge to the edge of the next draw where I blew the crow call a dozen times as loud as I could. I was almost blue in the face by the end of that series but it was worth it when we heard another gobble a few seconds later. The birds were already across the draw and on the next flat ridge, still moving away.

It went on like that for two hours and our only contact during that time was an occasional gobble in response to my crow calls, which by then were getting pretty tired, I admit. Still, as long as there was any hope, we had to keep trying.

In semi-open terrain like those rolling foothills I try to be careful whenever I start to cross a ridge or walk out on a flat. There's always a chance that you'll be seen by a turkey when you least expect it, and then the game really is over. Consequently, when we reached the crest of yet another hill where it flattened into a wide meadow, I peeked ahead carefully while the hunter waited a few yards behind. The sight of two black blobs pecking in the weeds less than a hundred yards away brought me to attention instantly.

"Jack, they're right there!" I hissed. "Back down the hill to those trees and we'll give them a try."

Jack sat against one tree in the shadows and I moved a few feet off to one side. When Jack was set, and his shotgun checked and loaded, I yelped a few times with the diaphragm, paused, and clucked a couple of times.

"Gobble-obble-obble!" They were coming and fast. I saw their craned heads, then fanned tails through the branches from my hiding spot and seconds later both birds were right in our laps. The blast of Jack's 12 gauge made my ears ring, but I didn't care. His 16 pound tom was flopping at our feet.

After it was all over, Jack, who had hunted turkeys a few times before without success, said, "I had no idea you could follow gobblers like that."

"Know something," I grinned, "neither did I." Come to think of it, I haven't done it quite that way since but I keep thinking that it worked once so the tactic may come in handy again someday, somewhere.

Noise makers do have their place, obviously, but there is such a thing as overkill. I do not rely on them as much these days as in the past simply because I'd rather hear a tom sound off on his own, meaning that if nothing else, I haven't disturbed him unnecessarily. When a bird does that he's acting naturally and hasn't a notion that he's got unexpected company.

These days, when I call loudly or resort to noise makers of one kind or another, it's usually because nothing else has worked and time is running out, or I'm trying to get a rise out of a turkey prior to the season so I'll know approximately where the birds are. Preseason scouting is a another ball game and I'll dwell on it a bit later on.

Chapter 6

Some Thoughts On Basic Equipment

One nice thing about turkey hunting, spring or fall, is that you really don't need an extensive array of equipment to tackle the chore. The basics are the same anywhere you go, East or West, with some regional variations in clothing, perhaps, due to the terrain and elements involved.

Cutting things to the bare minimum, you need a shotgun or bow, a turkey call or two, and the right clothing including raingear and comfortable footwear, and a small pack to tote necessities in when they aren't in use.

That's the very least, of course. Most turkey hunters acquire a longer list of "essentials" if for no other reason than because it's fun to experiment with new things, a realistic decoy, perhaps, or a new wonder call. Some of us also take some goodies along to make our stay in the woods more enjoyable and safe. In the West, where the density of turkey populations is generally not as great as in the East you may have to hike miles to hear a gobble so it pays to be prepared for any situation you're apt to encounter on a particular day.

Personally, I wear a small camouflaged daypack most of the time while hunting turkeys. In it I carry extra calls, a few rounds of ammunition, a couple of snacks, insect repellant, a flashlight, a compass, and a small first aid kit. I also have a knife, a piece of rope, toilet paper and, if it's going to be warm, water or fruit juice to drink. Rattlesnakes are a fact of life in some western areas so it's best to have a snakebite kit on hand, and I rarely go anywhere without the means to start a fire in case I get stuck somewhere unexpectedly.

In the West, where there's a considerable amount of open ground in some turkey areas, I rarely hunt without a pair of binoculars handy and I usually have them in the pack, as well. Another benefit of the daypack is the extra room for shed clothing when the chill of morning has turned to the heat of midday and the hike out is just beginning.

Some daypacks are designed for turkey hunting and include cushioned seats to make waiting that much more comfortable and sometimes even a large pouch for toting a gobbler when you get one. Packing a big bird out isn't all that difficult, true, but the typical legs first over-the-shoulder routine used most of the time, and illustrated in countless photographs in articles on turkey hunting, is hard on the shoulders if you're going very far. I've used a slip-on shotgun sling to carry turkeys occasionally, and honestly, if I'm traveling very far in rugged terrain in the future I'll be tempted to strap my daypack to a pack frame to which I can tie any gobbler later on.

A simple store bought turkey tote, or one you make at home especially for packing a big tom, or make on the spot for that matter, is nothing more than a short length of nylon rope tied to a handle a few inches long (a piece of antler perhaps, or thick dowling, or a smooth length of tree limb). You can grip the handle comfortably in front of your chest after tying the turkey's legs together with the rope and hoisting him over your shoulder. This is a comfortable way to carry a heavy bird but the rope will cut into your shoulder unless you pad it some way. There are also special game bags for turkey hunters, some in blaze orange, that will make carrying the load much easier.

To some extent, of course, the extras you carry will depend on the kind of hunting you expect to do. In some areas hunters have the luxury of being able to hunt turkeys close to home, of actually hunting for two or three hours before going to work. I can do that, but I've also driven hundreds of miles to a good spot. Occasionally, I've even backpacked into the woods overnight to be close to remote birds in the morning. In Montana, where ace Merriam's turkey hunter Rob Hazlewood lives, you might face a six hour drive to a real turkey haven like he does. In New Mexico you might want to hunt in the Gila Wilderness and it could take a string of pack horses to get you there. All that said, let's take a closer look at the basics of turkey hunting with a shotgun in hand. Bowhunting will be looked at in another chapter.

Anyway, turkeys are our biggest upland game birds. Adult hens may weigh 8 to 12 pounds. In the spring jakes will weigh anywhere from 11 to 17 pounds, depending perhaps on whether they were hatched early or late in the season and how well they've eaten during their first year. Most of the adult toms I've weighed ranged from 16 to 20 pounds with the majority somewhere in the 18 or 19 pound range. My biggest was a 24 pound Nebraska bird and I have a 21-1/2 pound

California tom that earned a permanent place under glass as a mounted trophy.

One way to pack a turkey is to use a turkey tote like Montana hunter Rob Hazlewood is doing here. His is a short length of rope tied to a deer antler handle.

The smallest wild turkey I ever killed was a fall hen poult that weighed just 9 pounds but was already as big as some adult Canada geese. Some really large toms reach 25 pounds and the biggest Merriam's gobbler listed in the 1985 Wild Turkey Records, compiled by the South Carolina based National Wild Turkey Federation, weighed 28 pounds. From the tip of the beak to the tip of his tail a mature tom measures 44-1/2 to 45 inches, according to my taxidermist friend Allan Jeffers, who receives turkeys to mount from different western states each year.

You get the picture, I'm sure. Wild turkeys are powerful birds with heavy feathering and long legs. They can fly strongly for short distances and glide for miles if necessary. Or they can run like race horses. Remember how hard it is to catch a wounded goose, with its short, churning legs? A wounded turkey will leave you in a cloud of dust.

The point is that you need an adequate shotgun for turkey hunting, and preferably one with a full choked barrel. Most hunters carry popular 12 gauge models and a few have turned to 10 gauge guns.

To pattern your shotgun at various ranges with different loads before hunting turkeys is a must. Here John Higley checks the results of a shot on a homemade turkey head target.

Some specialized turkey guns are now on the market, including Remington's Model 870 Special Purpose 12 gauge magnum models with a dull finish and interchangeable screw in chokes and a similar new shotgun by Winchester.

Some hunters, with more confidence in them than I have, feel that 20 gauge shotguns are heavy enough. It's not so much a matter of hitting power, as it is the amount of shot available per round, that makes me feel that my own 20 gauge pump is too light for the job. However, it doesn't chamber three inch shells which would make a difference, I'm sure.

It's the nature of the sport, especially in the spring, that most turkeys are called in and killed on the ground. Sometimes it's hard for a waterfowl or upland game hunter to understand that because they've been taught that taking all game birds in flight is where the sport comes in. But in spring turkey hunting, especially, and fall for that matter, there's real excitement in trying to dupe a gobbler and lure him to you, knowing all the while that any false move on your part will certainly spoil your act. Having a bird like that walk up looking for you, a living, talking decoy, is an exciting experience, and one that is ultimately addictive.

No matter what shotgun you use the object is to score clean kills rather than waste game, something every sportsman owes to any game. The most vulnerable part of a gobbler's anatomy is his exposed head and neck. Consequently, that's where experienced hunters aim. The rule to remember is this. If you just break a turkey's wing he can still run like mad, and if you hit him in the leg he may still be able to fly. If you hit him flush in the body while flying at close range you'll probably get your bird but I once saw a friend shoot a tom as it sailed over his head, and while the bird hit the ground hard, it recovered quickly and ran off before my friend could inject another shell in his pump and shoot again. That turkey was never found. Any turkey can be killed by a body hit if the shot penetrates deep enough into the vitals, but even so the bird may not die immediately and a wounded turkey can cover a lot of ground in a hurry.

From a purely practical standpoint, aiming only for the head and neck keeps most of the shot out of that delicious meat, as well.

Different hunters have different thoughts on just what the proper turkey loads are. They swear by anything from No.2 to No.7-1/2 shot and everything in between. In fact, even the small 7-1/2s will do the job, though they're only suited for close range, say 25 yards or less. Small pellets simply don't hit as hard at marginal ranges as heavier

45

Turkeys like this old gobbler have excellent eyesight and they are not colorblind—two reasons why hunters normally dress in head to toe camouflage.

shot and should be used only by someone with the willpower to wait for the right opportunity to present itself—which not all of us have. It should be noted that some states have established load margins. In California, for example, shot larger than No.2 may not be used for turkeys; some other states do not allow No.2s and a few do not allow 7-1/2s. Be sure to know the regulations wherever you are.

Since even a large turkey's head and neck represent an area smaller than your closed fist and thinner than your wrist, you need a fairly tight pattern. Most hunters use 2-3/4 inch or 3 inch magnum loads of No.4 or No.6 lead or copper plated shot. I started out with No.2 shot in the beginning, switched to No.4s somewhere along the way, and now swear by No.6s most of the time. There are also newly developed loads for turkeys that combine two different shot sizes— No.4s and No.6s for instance, but at realistic, sure kill turkey ranges I doubt that there's any advantage in mixing sizes.

This well dressed western turkey hunter blends in well with his surroundings.

My own change in shot size preference came after shooting my old 12 gauge pump at targets with a variety of loads and finding that No.6 shot out performed the rest out to 40 yards (as far as I'd ever want to shoot at a turkey) by a wide margin. It was downright scary to see how many, or rather how few, No.2s hit the vital area from that distance. I shudder to think that I used to use them all of the time. Since then I've come to realize a decided disadvantage to bigger shot, namely it can penetrate a turkey's vital organs at longer range with

Adequate footwear is an absolute must in the West where distances are long and rocks and cactus are sometimes plentiful.

no immediate visible effect. In other words you might mortally wound a bird that will get away only to die elsewhere.

Your shotgun may handle the various loads differently and may also have aiming characteristics not conducive to pointing directly at a target rifle style. In the interest of knowing what's going on, and feeling an added degree of confidence in your equipment, test fire your shotgun at homemade or store bought turkey head targets. You can make your own head and neck silhouettes out of paper strips roughly two inches wide (the neck size inside feathers and skin) by 12 inches long with a 3-1/2 inch rectangle on top representing the head. Mount the strips on large pieces of cardboard and shoot at them from measured distances. It's a real eye opener.

If you want to feel real sheepish in front of your hunter friends come back from a hunt someday and tell them you missed a big old tom at 24 yards because you didn't test your shotgun before the hunt.

"How do you miss a turkey?" is the first thing they'll ask. Trust me, I've owned up to a mistake or two like that myself I won't bore you with all the silly details but once I called an Oregon tom into easy range only to overshoot him badly with a borrowed shotgun. Later I even missed a target. Then I aimed a few inches low and riddled it. Happily, I got another chance at a Beaver State gobbler on a different day and redeemed myself somewhat—though I still get razzed on occasion.

48

Here's a true statement that might surprise you. You can wear practically any kind of clothing you want and still bag a turkey. At least one friend of mine used to do it all the time. Of course, there's a catch. To do that you have to be able to use natural cover as well as an old buck—the kind that always seems to disappear into the woodwork as soon as the season opens. In some crowded eastern areas, in fact, there's been talk about requiring some sort of blaze orange apparel for turkey hunting because there are so many hunters. Since safety is so important it will be discussed in depth later on.

A California hunter sets his decoy out where he hopes a tom will see it.

As for clothing, though, most experienced turkey hunters consider camouflage to be the best choice because it helps you to blend in with your surroundings. A turkey's senses of hearing and vision are

49

keen. Their eyesight, especially, saves many of them from the roasting pan every year, spring or fall. Turkeys seem to spot movement instantly and they are not colorblind. If they could smell you like a deer, you'd need a pocket full of four leafed clover to kill one.

A turkey responding to a call is all eyes. Even when he advances quickly he always looks for anything suspect, and that can include some bright part of your clothing. The way a turkey seems to study everything you might think they can see through any disguise. You feel half naked if you happen to wear light socks and your pants raise up to expose them when you sit down. The same disquieting feeling is present if your hands and face are exposed.

This Montana Merriam's tom is completely fooled by a homemade decoy.
(Bill Thomas photo)

Camouflage, then, gives a hunter the confidence to sit only partly concealed while a tom comes into range. I used to wear blue jeans with a camo shirt or poncho and sit behind a low screen of brush to hide my legs. In complete camo I can now choose a stand with fewer obstructions between me and an approaching gobbler, and that's an obvious advantage because I have a better field of view. When hunting any critter that seems to be all eyes the ability to remain still is paramount, and even when you don't move a muscle you plain feel better in camo than otherwise.

Wear a camouflage shirt and pants, or coveralls, and a camo jacket or rain poncho, if necessary. In the West, where it's not uncommon to begin the day in near freezing temperatures, and end it in bright sunlight, I often wear an insulated vest and long underwear under my outer clothes to start, knowing that I can always take a layer off and stuff it in my daypack if the temperature rises later. I also feel more secure wearing lightweight brown, green or camo colored gloves rather than hunting bare handed. The actual camo pattern doesn't make much difference, by the way, as long as the colors don't clash too much with the background. Shades of green are good in the spring woods and I've worn both leaf and bark patterns with good results.

To complete my camo outfit I sometimes wear a headnet or face mask to hide my head. I wear glasses, however, and find they fog over from body heat under a mask, and that camo cream is a better answer under those conditions. Some hunters even grow a beard for turkey hunting and shield their eyes with their hat brim. Lastly, if your shotgun has a shiny finish it's a good idea to at least cover the barrel with a strip of camo tape. My newest "turkey gun" is a 12 gauge Remington Model 870 SP Magnum so the dull finish is built in already.

Footwear, of course, is important, but, really, leather boots blend in well enough for most hunting purposes. When it's wet, though, I wear pacs or waterproof rubber boots with a sole design that affords good traction for climbing hills when necessary. Some of the ankle high Gore-Tex boots now available (some come in camo colors) are excellent for basic turkey hunting, especially if you have to cover a lot of ground and weight is a consideration.

One more thing that qualifies as basic equipment for many hunters these days is some sort of decoy. There are full bodied plastic, inflatable and silhouette types on the market and all of them work when the circumstances are right. Decoys serve to divert a tom's attention from your calling position and they may, in some cases, be the convincer needed to draw a reluctant tom in close enough for a shot. They do not always work and they are not always necessary, but I use one at times, and so do many turkey hunters I know. The problem, of course, is that you've got to carry the decoy around with you all day, unless you have a place to stash it, and that can be bothersome.

Offhand, I think a decoy is most useful at daybreak, especially if you're able to place it where a tom might see it immediately after pitching down from his roost, and perhaps in a roosting area in the late afternoon where a tom might be looking for company before flying up in the evening. The trend these days is to use more than one decoy (I know a guy who used 6 one morning) but most of my successful hunter friends don't use them at all, with the exception of some bowhunters I know.

So, take your pick. Like anything else decoys will not solve your turkey hunting problems if you do not put the rest of the facets of the hunt in perspective. Sometimes they work, sometimes they don't. They are fun to try once in awhile but they are not medicine for all the moods of a wary gobbler or a panacea for all the troubles the average turkey hunter has.

Chapter 7

Spring Fever In The West

It is April somewhere in the West. In your state the annual spring turkey season has just gotten underway and you're anxious to go. It has been a long winter, as most are, but now the promise of spring fills the air. In the mountains even a recent snow storm doesn't keep the deciduous trees from starting to bud. In the lowlands wildflowers are starting to sprout and tender new grass greens the hills.

You leave the driveway of your home or motel at 3 a.m., or perhaps you just stir around camp. As you head for the hunting spot you glance upward. If you're lucky a few million stars wink back. Very little breeze is stirring. It will be a good day for gobbling, you think, a very good day, indeed.

After driving for awhile you park beside the winding road and prepare to hike along a ridge on a muddy skid trail. The fingers of your gloved right hand are wrapped around the familiar shape of your favorite "turkey gun", perhaps a battered 12 gauge pump with a full choked barrel. Soon your sweat is flowing but the air is downright cold. You shudder at the thought of how you'll shiver when you finally reach the spot where you intend to wait for dawn. For an instant you actually long for the warm bed you left behind, but you shake off such musings by thinking about the turkeys somewhere in the woods nearby.

Turkeys. It's hard to explain your feelings about them and if you try non-hunters will look away uncomfortably, as if they were being approached by an over zealous used car salesman while walking by the lot. Turkeys are mere poultry to them, something mass produced on farms they never see, birds with a reputation for stupidity, meat usually bought already plucked and wrapped just before Thanksgiving.

You may remember dimly a time when you felt the same way but turkey hunting has turned you into a believer. Wild turkeys are something special. They're wary, cautious, suspicious, boisterous, spectacular and exciting. Whether or not they're actually smart is debatable, but they're awfully good at doing whatever it is that wild turkeys do, and they're more than challenging enough for you.

Many hunters in your state are new to turkey hunting, and you are really just learning because there's no long standing tradition of the sport in many western areas. Already, however, you suspect that a hunter never really knows it all. No one really knows what a turkey's going to do next, though your educated guesses are striking home more often. You smile to yourself, all alone in the dark. Man, it is fun!

To be successful at turkey hunting you have to sink your teeth into the sport. It's more than just looking or listening, more than finding quail with a pointing dog, or flushing pheasants. Turkey hunting involves you completely, on a scale rarely reached in any other bird hunting including waterfowling, and that's especially true in the spring.

You realize this is not the sport for groups of hunting buddies, even the guys you chase deer or elk with. There are exceptions, of course. You do tolerate, even enjoy, a partner once in awhile, especially a kid born to hunt, or a best friend, but once in awhile greed sets in and you have to sneak away alone. Only you and the turkeys. You succeed or fail on your own, with no one to blame but yourself when you aren't patient enough to wait out a tom that you don't think is coming in— but is. No one to blame but yourself when a hen walks right up and looks you in the eye and "putts" with alarm when your elbow slips off your knee and your shotgun barrel sags, thus scaring her, and the tom you know is somewhere behind her, into deathly silence. Certainly, hunting solo has its advantages when you accidently practice catch-and-release turkey hunting, but it also adds to your chance of success by eliminating the possible mistakes of others.

In the spring only gobblers are taken. The proven theory behind such hunting is that there are always more toms than necessary in any healthy flock. Dominant males breed with as many hens as possible. If one boss is killed, another tom will usually fill in. Regardless, enough breeding activity normally takes place before most spring seasons begin to assure a good supply of poults during a normal nesting season.

Biologically, then, there are usually more than enough toms to deem quite a few as excess. In fact, if every tom was killed during the spring—unlikely at best—half the poults hatched that season would be males, thus assuring an ample number for the following spring. Rooster only pheasant hunting is based on the same criteria.

The real challenge of spring turkey hunting lays in calling a gobbler into close range like this California hunter has done.

Like most hunting, turkey hunting is what you make it. You hear about hunters who turn to stalking or ambush when calling doesn't produce, and while there might be a place for such tactics in some rare cases, the most fun, and the real challenge in hunting spring gobblers, lays in calling them into shotgun or bow and arrow range. With a shotgun close enough is about 40 yards, or less. With a bow, 20 yards is more like it.

Hunters with a reputation for success are sometimes envied or regarded as gurus by those new to the sport. But, while such "experts" obviously understand what they're doing, the ingredients for success are not above anyone with the desire to succeed.

It's true. Practically anyone can call a turkey. After all, I do it all of the time, and while I feel I know what makes them (turkeys) turn on—part of the time anyway—no one would accuse me of calling with flawless precision. In fact, I sound terrible at times, but then, so do the turkeys. I do not mean to sell the ability to call well short because that's something to take pride in, but you do not have to be perfect to talk turkey effectively.

When I first started hunting turkeys I did things because I read about them, or was told by someone else that I ought to do this or that. Some of the things suggested seemed like miracle cures for hunting woes but, really, nothing works all of the time in turkey hunting, and some days nothing works at all. That is, of course, part of the fun and challenge, the difference between hunting and killing.

In the beginning I read that every turkey hunter worth his salt got into the woods well before daybreak. All of the articles said so. But why?

Well, to begin with the crack of dawn is simply a great time to be outdoors. If things go accordingly the coming sunrise will wake the forest critters up at around the same time. Even before it's light an old tom might start gobbling from his roost, and other toms in the area will usually join in. They're telling each other, and any hens in the vicinity, just where they are, though there might be hens in the same trees with them.

Normally the hens will go to a tom shortly after they fly down, and sometimes the tom will see them before he leaves his roost. But if the hens and toms don't get together promptly, perhaps because they roosted in separate locations, the toms may get anxious and go looking for company as soon as they're on the ground. If you happen to be nearby and a tom hears you calling he may come right in. Then again, he may not. There are days, in fact, when a tom might gobble only once, or not at all, and go on his merry way without paying attention to you. There are many factors at work during any turkey hunt including weather and wind conditions, hunting pressure in a particular area, unexpected encounters with the gobblers you're trying to locate, and the disposition of the hens on a particular morning. More on these, and other things, in Tough Turkey.

Occasionally, however, things go just right at dawn, as they did for

John Higley says practically anyone can call a turkey like this fine Rio Grande/Merriam's hybrid from California. After all, he does it all the time.

me recently on a dewey spring morning in the northern California hills.

An hour before daylight I worked my way down a long oak dotted ridge with a flashlight in hand until I was about 250 yards from the spot where I thought some turkeys would be roosting. Just in case, and because I could hear into other areas from a vantage point, I chose to wait quietly in the dark until I heard a tom gobble voluntarily. Since I knew the country I figured I could still get into position before he left his roost no matter where he was.

57

The first gobble came as a faint crack of light appeared in the east. It told me exactly where that turkey was, and probably some of his buddies, too. I moved in quickly and sat down against a blue oak several yards behind a line of manzanita that screened my approach. At least three noisy toms were now sounding off periodically and I was only about 100 yards away, plenty close enough for them to hear the softest calls I could make.

A few minutes before fly down time I let the toms know where I was by yelping quietly, like a hen just greeting the dawn (some hunters call them tree yelps but hens do the same thing on the ground at times). Regardless, the idea was to get the attention of the gobblers and one lustful response after another told me it worked. I repeated the call two or three times then clammed up and listened for the birds to leave the pine trees they were in.

Presently I heard feathers hitting branches as the birds came down and soon a couple of ground level gobbles told me the toms were walking. At the same time I became aware of several hens around me and I wondered if I stood a chance with such competition. I yelped loudly six or seven times, clucked a bit, and yelped again. And then I sensed a pattern forming. Some hens were now in the open meadow where the toms landed, but one gobbler seemed to be getting closer to me. He didn't gobble often but I could swear I heard him strut and puff. I called softly, like a hen feeding away, and prayed.

I saw his bluish-white head first, then his fanned tail feathers, and felt my heart racing the 440. The tom walked behind a bush and I brought my weathered pump gun up. When he stepped clear he raised his head, looking for the bogus hen, and my shot still echoes somewhere across the valley of time.

That bird, which fell just 18 yards away, had all the makings of a boss gobbler, the one to which most of the hens would have gone eventually. I saw other toms in the area later but they weren't as big. The old monarch weighed 21 pounds, had a beard 10-7/8s inches long, and spurs nearly an inch in length.

That's why you go into the woods early. You hear more turkey noise just before and after daybreak, and toms without hens, or toms simply looking for hens they think they hear, are most susceptible to an imposter's calls at that time. However, if things don't go right at first, being there early gives you several more potentially productive hours to hunt before the usual early morning flurry of gobbling activity tapers off.

When all goes right you will end your western hunt with a fine tom on your shoulder like this nice Wyoming gobbler taken by Ron Dube.

Rob Hazelwood shows the end result of a perfect spring morning hunt in Montana—a beautiful, mature Merriam's gobbler.

But no matter what time it is when you talk turkey, gobblers like the old fellow just mentioned are the cause and cure (temporarily, of course) of spring fever in the West.

60

Chapter 8

Tough Turkey

There are days in western turkey hunting when everything goes just right. In fact, after some hunts are over, and you're hiking out with a tom over your shoulder, you might smugly think to yourself, there's nothing to it. If you've hunted turkeys very often, however, you know the easy toms come at a cost of several that did everything in the world to frustrate you. If you think about it, you realize that many gobblers qualify as "tough turkeys" and some are downright impossible. Often the difference between a successful and an unsuccessful hunter is simply a matter of dedication.

The guy who doesn't get discouraged when problems arise, and tries to figure out why a particular tom did a certain thing on a particular day, is usually the one who reaps the rewards eventually.

Western turkeys are tough for many reasons and terrain is obviously one of them.

For a couple of seasons I guided turkey hunters on a northern California ranch and hunting preserve. There was a fair population of Rio Grande turkeys on the 40,000 acre property but the area they inhabited was a network of rugged, roadless canyons. The terrain alone made hunting difficult and I realized early on the importance of knowing where the birds roosted the night before if my hunter for the day was going to have any chance at all of bagging a tom.

The birds normally used specific parts of the deepest canyon where there was a year round stream bordered by impenetrable berry vines, poison oak, and large sycamore, cottonwood and oak trees. A half mile wide and 900 feet deep, the canyon was laced with rimrocks and a man had to know exactly where to go or he couldn't get down. I would get to the canyon rim late in the afternoon, armed with binoculars, mosquito repellant and patience. Eventually I would see or hear the turkeys moving down a ridge somewhere and by watching which direction they flew, and listening for a tom to gobble good night, I could plan the next morning's attack.

Because of the nature of the terrain it was imperative to learn every inch of the landscape in advance of a hunt. Without a helicopter there was simply no way to cross the canyon quickly, and heading the turkeys off on the opposite hillside was impossible. In some places you couldn't hike across at all and even the turkeys commonly flew to get around, easily leaving any hunter behind. At the same time, the turkeys were actually very vulnerable once you knew the lay of the land. They always began their morning assembly in the same park-like openings, depending on where they roosted the evening before, and if you got set up in the right spot you could almost count on bagging a tom shortly after fly down time.

Jim Zumbo with a big eastern Wyoming tom he took after following the bird to the far side of a deep gorge. The turkey flew, Jim hiked, and his effort paid off.

In April, 1990, outdoor writer Jim Zumbo and I encountered Merriam's turkeys in the Black Hills of eastern Wyoming that acted much like those California birds. Even though we didn't know the country very well on our first visit there, I recognized the situation as being very similar to those ranch hunts. When the turkeys didn't hesitate to fly across a steep gorge I knew they did it all the time. We looked at a map, found a way to get across ourselves by a roundabout route, and called in an anxious round tail tom for Jim a few hours later.

Some hunters, hearing turkeys fly away from an area like that, might think the birds were spooked. In some cases, however, they're just doing what comes naturally to western birds in canyon country.

Of course, there are other barriers that effect turkeys and turkey hunters everywhere including fences, creeks, ponds, draws and even open meadows that they won't readily cross at times.

Fences are a nuisance that can cause problems that some hunters aren't aware of. Much western ranch country is laced with barbed wire barriers, many of which have hog wire mesh on the bottom half, and while turkeys are perfectly capable of flying over a fence when they can't slip through somewhere, they usually don't do so readily. Instead they follow the fence or pace back and forth along it. A tom may "hang up" and gobble at a hen or hunter calling on the other side until he's joined by the real thing or gets suspicious, or tired, and slips away.

Knowing where the fences are in advance is advantageous. I recall one bright morning when I heard a distant tom on the other side of a shallow draw bisecting a plateau. He gobbled voluntarily so I closed the gap between us quickly, making sure I wasn't skylined along the way. When I thought I was close enough I found a place to sit and yelped a few times with a box call. The answer was immediate, and the tom was closer than I expected. Boy, he's going to come right in, I thought, and pointed my shotgun in his general direction.

"Gobble-obble-obble, gobble-obble-obble!" He double gobbled and triple gobbled at my every yelp. He was firecracker hot. The tom wanted company, and I wanted to give it to him, but suddenly I realized he was walking back and forth and not coming any closer. It hit me like a hammer would a gong, only quieter. Fence!

Taking a chance that I'd be seen, I took off toward the gobbler again. Luckily he was slightly above me and out of view when I spotted the barrier and ducked down 20 yards from it beside a boulder. I clucked with the box, put it down, and raised my shotgun

Knowing where the fences are in a particular area is advantageous. Turkeys sometimes follow such barriers back and forth rather than simply flying over them.

again. A throaty, "Where are you?" yelp reached my ears, then a gobble rang out. In seconds the tom was in view—and boy, was he ever in range.

Another tom, with which I became very familiar, acted much the same way and the barrier he wouldn't cross was a small creek. He could have flown it easily, and a different bird might have done just that, but not this one. I got him by moving in close, which isn't always possible of course, and waiting for him to wander down by the water again.

It would be great if all problems were simply the result of terrain variations, or barriers of one kind or another, but that would be too easy. Turkeys everywhere react to calling in many similar ways, and sometimes that means not reacting at all. They can be both easy to dupe and hard to entice. They may ignore your every pleading yelp, or come running, and it's hard to figure why. But while hard answers may be difficult to come by, a hunter luckily doesn't have to know all of them to be successful.

For some reason turkeys will often refuse to cross even small streams like this when responding to a call.

More than anything else, what a tom does on a particular morning depends on what the hens in the vicinity do. Hens are conditioned to go to a gobbler for breeding, which makes sense because turkeys do not pair like geese or quail, and toms breed with as many hens as possible during the mating period, which lasts for several weeks. If toms always had to race around looking for the loose hens they'd run themselves ragged in short order. The fact that the toms will come to a hunter's calls at times is proof that lust and loneliness can overrule the normal order of things.

As the breeding season approaches the toms re-establish dominance by fighting and threatening one another. Actually this is an ongoing process that begins shortly after the turkeys are hatched. The search for dominance is carried on somewhat all through their lives but it intensifies in the spring. Jakes, being younger and smaller than adult toms, usually will not tangle with the older gobblers, but apparently there are exceptions and I've seen jakes alone with hens a number of times. Maybe it was because there weren't any bigger males in that particular location and maybe dominance is more the result of an individual tom's aggressive attitude than size.

In any event jakes without hens are very susceptible to calling, perhaps because they're uneducated and less wary than some older toms, and many turkey hunting memories are built around them. Admittedly, it's a thrill to bag a long bearded old gobbler, but any tom turkey that responds to a call is a worthy quarry.

Anyway, how gobblers respond to calling varies much of the time according to what the hens are doing, and where they are at a particular time. When hens are nearby, or actually with a tom, getting him to come your way can be a real problem. It's my impression, actually, that when hens and toms are roosting together the hens often ignore or deliberately shy away from the calls they hear on the ground. The toms, seeing the real hens go one way, are more apt to follow than respond to a fake somewhere in the brush.

You can hear it happen, but you can't do much about it. You'll hear a tom gobbling up a storm in a roost tree, then he'll fly down, gobble a couple more times as if to say, "Over here honey," to you, and shut up completely. That usually means he's with the hens and is busy breeding, and doesn't have any time to come for you. Oh, he might continue to gobble sporadically, but he's telling you to come on over, and eventually he'll walk away, knowing instinctively that any hen worth his trouble will catch up.

This situation is not impossible but it can be frustrating and I'm not quite sure why it happens; so the theory I'm about to advance is only conjecture at this time and subject to change at any moment. Fact is, there is a pecking order among hens as there is gobblers. It could be that the dominant hen is treating you like one of her followers or simply doesn't want the competition from an outsider. She knows you'll tag along if you're a member of the group so she's not going to bow to you and because the lead hen goes one way the others will too and the tom(s) won't be far behind. That said, there are times when you might get the upper hand by challenging the lead hen with a series of "cuts" and making her come to the interloper to show her who's boss.

Custom gunstock maker Ed Sweet of Meridian, Idaho is one of that state's most successful turkey hunters. That isn't surprising, perhaps, because Ed is originally from Pennsylvania where some 300,000 spring turkey hunters take their sport very seriously, indeed. To Ed, Idaho toms seem pretty easy to dupe once the scouting is done but he still encounters trouble when the hens are with the toms. As I indicated at least twice before in this chapter the presence of hens is always a troublesome, if natural, part of turkey hunting. You can overcome the situation occasionally, however, and reap the rewards of success.

"That's when I do a lot of hard, raspy cutting to get the dominant hen worked up hoping she'll come in to investigate. If it works the whole flock, including the tom(s) will be along shortly," Ed told me.

On the other hand all the hard, raspy calling in the world won't work all the time or it might bring unexpected results. Often there's more than one tom with a group of hens including the boss gobbler and his subordinate hangers-on. While the boss keeps an eye on the flock you might play the part of a stray hen and lure a lustful subordinate tom away from the group. That term makes a subordinate tom sound puny but that isn't always the case. He can be just as big as the boss but a little less energetic this week, or this season, for one reason or another.

When a turkey is coming to a call his keen eyesight, is his most important asset, but merely being silent makes a tom you've located disappear in an instant. Sometimes a tom will gobble only once before leaving the roost in the morning, or he may not gobble at all. It may mean he's with hens already, or it may mean he doesn't have the urge to breed that day, or that he's sneaking in silently to you. Perhaps it's windy and you couldn't hear him anyway. Maybe a storm front's moving in and effecting his urges, resulting in what some hunters refer to as a no gobble day. The toms simply do not sound off, but they are probably a lot closer than you think.

A stiff wind is probably the worst weather condition a hunter has to face. If it's raining hard, or snowing, I have the good sense to stay in bed most of the time. But when it's windy and clear I'm always tempted to go to it despite the inevitably poor results. I think the wind worries turkeys, makes them spooky, and if they gobble you probably won't be able to hear them. In fact, I don't think the turkeys can hear each other very well in such conditions unless they're in a protected canyon or basin. Sometimes the worst wind will die down by late afternoon, however, and it may be calm for an hour or two in the morning so what the heck, take a chance.

Heavy rain may cause turkeys to stay on their roosts until late in the morning and I've seen toms hanging onto a ponderosa pine limb at 8 a.m. when a storm was in progress. I do like to hunt on the morning when a storm is breaking up, if it isn't very windy, and I've had good luck on such days. I'll go out in light, misty rain, as opposed to a gully washer, as well, because the turkeys will usually go about their business normally on such days.

I remember one misty morning a few years ago when I hiked to a favorite spot in the dark and waited on a skid road overlooking a

Turkeys are effected by the elements, such as rain, wind or snow but more than anything, what a tom will do on a particular day is dictated by the behavior of the neighborhood hens.

basin for one of the toms in the area to sound off. There wasn't a peep by daybreak so I started walking, looking for fresh sign, and calling and listening into other draws. Presently, I found several soft droppings, so I knew there were birds nearby, but it wasn't until 9 o'clock or so that a lone hen yelped back to my calls. She walked right by the bush where I was sitting and I watched her eating manzanita blossoms as she went up the hill. Later I walked around a corner and flushed another turkey. It was big and dark bodied and even in the low overcast gloom I felt sure it was a gobbler.

It rained and snowed lightly all day but the next morning I was back, and while the trees were still dripping, there were also a few starry holes in the clouds. I knew I'd see the sun off and on at daybreak. Without realizing it I then got lucky. I stopped on the same overlook I usually use and tried to make the tom gobble by howling like a coyote in the dark. That didn't work so I just sat there waiting for the gobbler to wake up on his own. Meanwhile, a hen, most likely the same one I saw the day before, was roosted just above and behind me in a tall pine and I didn't know it. As soon as she could see she took off in a huff and, besides giving me a start, she sailed clear across the drainage to the next mountainside, about half a mile away.

Hearing nothing for another half hour, I started searching again. Eventually, I wound up in the same spot where I'd seen the hen the day before and when I yelped half heartedly with a diaphragm, from the same bush where I waited for the hen, a gobble from around the hill sent a shiver up my spine. To make a long story short, a still damp and somewhat bedraggled tom walked, and strutted, into view a few minutes later and I gladly took the 18 pounder home with me. Persistence won another round.

Bumping into that hen was purely an accident and had nothing to do with planning on my part. I'm sure I would have had difficulty had she been closer to the tom and the fact that I flushed him the day before may have worked in my favor by separating him from the hen to begin with.

Northern Californian Cliff Dewell, who hunts turkeys constantly with both a bow and shotgun, had a similar, but slightly different, experience that's worth re-telling. Cliff is also a little fanatical and doesn't know enough to stay in bed when the weather's only moderately poor. On one particular morning it was raining lightly and Cliff didn't hear a turkey sound in an area where he knew there were several toms.

"I hunted there often," he told me, "and I kept seeing this hen on

Even on the best of days gobbling activity usually tapers off by mid-morning. However, where it's allowed, even late afternoon hunting can pay off like this.

the point of a little hill. Usually I heard a tom or two there, too, so when everything else failed I decided to wait where the hen usually was and see what might happen."

What happened is that Cliff called softly every once in awhile with a favorite slate call, and eventually he heard the haunting sound of a tom strutting. He put the slate aside and picked his shotgun up and was ready when the silent tom walked into view a few minutes later. It seems apparent that Cliff's earlier observations of the hen helped him put two and two together on a tough turkey day.

A tom that shuts up suddenly effectively disappears, but that doesn't necessarily mean he's gone anywhere. Some toms sneak into a call quietly and you can't overlook that option. However, most are simply busy with hens they can see, for the time being anyway. I've spent a lot of mornings in the woods without hearing much turkey talk, or any at all, and a few of those times I've come home with fine toms anyway because I stayed with it.

Even on a morning when toms seem to be gobbling everywhere the noise generally tapers off after a few hours. By then many of the toms have been joined by hens and most breeding activity is completed. That's when most hunters leave the woods, even though the shooting hours aren't over by any means. In fact, you can hunt all day in the spring in some western states, such as Montana, Idaho, Wyoming and New Mexico, while half day hunting is the norm in others like California.

At some point during the season a hen will usually start her clutch of eggs. That means that sometime during the morning she will probably leave the tom she's with to lay an egg in her nest, a process she may repeat daily for two weeks. Individual hens may or may not join up with the toms again later in the day.

As usual many variables are at work. Not all hens start their nests at the same time and some incubating hens show up again after losing their clutch of eggs to predators or other calamities such as flooding or human interference. Regardless, the number of hens in evidence usually diminishes as the season progresses and a tom may suddenly be very lonely, and start gobbling again when his remaining hens depart, if only temporarily, to visit their nests.

If a tom does lose his hens in midmorning you may be right on top of a good situation if you're still in the woods. It doesn't always happen but more than once I've been taking a break in a spot of sunlight, usually eating a candy bar snack, when a gobbler opened up suddenly in the distance after hours of silence.

One day when that happened Phil Grunert and I sat fascinated as a hen sauntered by on her way to the nest, and while the deserted tom gobbled voluntarily time and time again, he never moved an inch. It wasn't too long before the hen walked by us in the opposite direction and as soon as she reached the tom the woods were deathly quiet again. Phil and I were in a bad place and we couldn't move closer or try calling from another spot. The tom answered our every yelp but he was determined to hold his ground until his hen returned which, of course, she did. Other times, though, hearing a late morning gobble or two paid off nicely.

A single gobble alerted me one sunny morning when I was halfway finished with a Snickers bar. The sound was a long way off so I slipped my daypack on and hurried across gullies and over rolling hills until I worried that I'd gone too far. I yelped tentatively with my box call and a lusty reply told me the tom was above me in a little basin. I circled around the sound until coming to the lip of the depression where I got set up and called softly a few times. Suddenly, I saw one hen hiking up the slope behind the basin and another jogged by to my right. By now the tom was gobbling repeatedly and it only took another cluck or two to convince him I was the real thing. His beard was nearly 10 inches long.

I've always felt that a tom heard in mid-morning is quite susceptible to calling. The ironic thing is that most hunters don't stick it out that long.

In the open terrain typical of many places in the West, and some spots in the East, as well, heavily hunted toms become highly suspicious of hens they can hear but can't see. They will not usually cross too much exposed ground and they are more apt to gobble and display in the distance, expecting to attract the hen to them. If she doesn't show eventually the tom may simply walk away.

Or he may decide to come a little closer like a fine old tom did for California guide Chuck Harrison awhile back.

Chuck first heard that bird in a draw on the edge of a plateau in basically wide open terrain. As he explained it, he couldn't get close to the bird, and the tom certainly could have seen any hen within a quarter mile. When Chuck yelped with his box the tom went into full strut and walked behind some brush, gobbling repeatedly.

"He was definitely interested in finding another hen," Harrison mused later, "but he wanted her to come to him in the worst way. When she didn't, he couldn't stand it and started coming closer, but he was in no hurry at all and everytime he stopped it was behind a bush where he all but disappeared. We finally got him but it took more than an hour for him to come 200 yards. I don't call birds like that dumb!"

I've already mentioned persistence and dedication and I'll probably cover them again in one way or another before finishing this

California hunter Chuck Harrison harvested this nice Rio Grande tom after coaxing the tom for more than an hour. In other words, he didn't give up as long as there was any hope at all.

book. Fact is, there are several things involved in turkey hunting success including calling and scouting (finding a place to hunt where there are some birds) and persistence and dedication are right at the top of the list, too.A hunter with those qualities is unlikely to become discouraged when he draws a blank one or more days in a row.

It is true that even a newcomer to the sport of wild turkey hunting can get lucky right off the bat, and while I say more power to him, I hope he doesn't think it will be that easy all the time. Many elements enter the turkey's world everyday, and how a tom reacts to them determines whether or not he'll be easy, tough or impossible. The fun is in trying to figure out why a glorified chicken does what it does and to beat him at his own game, even if it's a game he doesn't really know he's playing in the first place.

Turkeys are survivors, however. The more hunting pressure there is the more wary and nervous they become. They naturally have to contend with predators and I have no doubt that during part of the year, at least, human beings head their list of things to avoid.

Chapter 9

The Hunt

There are many unseen facets to the sport of wild turkey hunting, especially as viewed by someone unfamiliar with the pastime. I have seen knowledgeable big game hunters, for instance, who were good at stalking four legged game but who were nonetheless careless as far as turkey hunting is concerned. To them, perhaps, a game bird was a game bird, but turkeys are really different than all the rest. Most of the hunters would learn, of course, but for the time being their movements in the woods were such that any turkey that wasn't blind would see them first and probably depart without ever being noticed.

But what does how you move through the woods have to do with hiding and calling an old gobbler in, anyway? A lot, I think. In the West covering lots of ground is normally a big part of the game and you never know when you're going to bump into a tom unexpectedly during daylight hours, when you're simply hiking from one spot to another. There are also times when you'll hear a distant tom after daybreak that you know you have to get closer to. Closing the gap, to reach a practical calling position, usually takes a special touch and that's where the right technique comes in.

Think about it for a moment. A turkey has excellent eyesight and a big tom with his neck outstretched stands about 30 inches high so he can see over obstacles that might hide his body completely. And yet he can still see under the lower branches of the oaks and pines common to many open western forests. Consequently, he might see you, or part of your anatomy, and even if he doesn't know what you are, he knows better than to stick around and gawk.

Obviously, you're going to bump into some toms accidently no matter what you do but you can avoid such things once in awhile by staying on your toes and using the terrain to your best advantage. In other words don't walk the top of a ridge in plain sight in the midst of a hunt unless you can keep far enough back from the edge to stay out of view of any turkey(s) on the slopes below. Rather than approaching a noisy tom directly, while looking for a spot from which to call, deliberately make use of land contours, shadows and clumps of brush if necessary.

Before we go on let me clarify one point. Once again I've mentioned moving on a tom, something that is often necessary for success. I want to make it clear here, however, that changing positions, or trying to get closer, does not mean stalking a tom and trying to get in range for a shot. Not only does that not work very often, it's a dangerous and unnecessary tactic, as we will see later in the chapter on safety and ethics.

Years ago I commonly walked the open ridges, calling sporadically, in the hope of raising a gobble somewhere along the way, without paying much attention to my position when I started yelping. Now, with more experience under my camo hat, I rarely call until I'm aware of a spot to set up in just in case I get a sudden response from a tom nearby. In other words, I try to stay ready at all times, and that's easier said than done when the hours drag on and fatigue sets in.

As usual, though, I don't always follow my own advice. One nice spring morning, for instance, Phil Grunert and I heard more than one tom walk out of the northern California canyon we were in and head for the top of a wide, oak dotted flat. We went after them but the turkeys weren't being especially vocal, for reasons known only to themselves, and we eventually called ourselves silly without locating the toms again. Finally, we decided to float a few yelps into the canyon just once more from the edge of the flat, but by that time we were getting tired and careless and we just stood there in the grass, wildflowers and rocks, and yelped loudly down the hill as we looked out over the spring green country.

No one was more surprised than us when we heard the quizzical, throaty yelps of a tom a minute or two later, and realized he was directly behind us and coming steadily our way. I turned my eyes toward Phil and saw him looking back with a sheepish grin spreading across his face. We were caught and we knew it, and an instant later the tom took off like the biggest quail you ever saw. He was gone before either of us could think to shoot.

That incident reminded me of the time a friend and I were hunting pronghorn antelope in Wyoming and it was his first try. He was an experienced deer hunter but being new at the game he didn't realize just how well pronghorns could see. When we got near the crest of the hill we were climbing, to glass into the basin on the other side, I dropped to my knees and started crawling toward a clump of brush to hide my approach. But my friend walked right up to the top, despite my frantic gestures, and a fine buck antelope, maybe 600 yards away, took off in a beeline for Utah. When my friend finally learned to respect a pronghorn's vision he made a beautiful stalk and killed a fine buck. When a turkey hunter takes care not to expose himself unnecessarily his success also improves noticeably.

As a general rule of thumb it's good to call to a tom when you're on his level or above him somewhat. Like anything, however, there are unavoidable variables that dictate to you what your options are. Calling to some toms from above might mean from the top of a cliff so you've got to play it by ear, so to speak, and adjust to the situation at hand. Most of the time you should be at the tom's level or slightly above but if you can't, try him from below and you might be pleasantly surprised. I remember calling more than one gobbler down a steep mountainside right into my lap so it can be done.

I use binoculars a lot in open western terrain and sometimes spot turkeys from afar even when I don't hear them.

Calling position is always important. It's best to set up with a view of an opening, which can be anything from a small meadow to an abandoned road. The idea is to be able to see a tom when he gets close enough and not to be in brush so thick that it blocks your view too much. This is another lesson learned the hard way, which seems to be the only way I absorb things.

One time I heard a tom answer my pleading yelps as I walked along a two track road in the California foothills. With the bird's second gobble I realized he was coming right to me so I ducked around a corner, got into the manzanita brush, and snuggled up against the trunk of a big one. I could see part of a log landing and expected the tom to come far enough to strut his stuff for the hen he thought was there. What he did, instead, was cut straight across the road into the brush off to my left, where he gobbled repeatedly for several minutes as I sat, just out of view, maybe 15 yards away.

This calling position might work but it's a poor choice. When possible, it's far better to sit against a form breaking barrier such as a large tree trunk with a clear view ahead and to the sides.

He gobbled enough, actually, to attract two hens which sauntered by me less than 10 yards away and went right to him. That should have been the end of it but the turkeys weren't quite finished with me. A few minutes later the hens walked across the landing and the tom followed along like a trained puppy. He had his back toward me and his round tail was fully fanned so I couldn't see his head at all and I didn't shoot. I still don't know why it didn't dawn on me to just make an odd noise, whereby his head would have come up in a flash.

Two lessons in one day. Had I simply watched the old road from the outside edge of the brush I would have seen the tom come across, and had I the sense to startle him somehow when his back was turned I would have had time for a shot. I had enough sense not to shoot at his rear end because that would have made a mess of a fine trophy and a lot of meat, but I didn't have the presence of mind to do anything to change his attitude and make him stick his head up.

However, I've never forgotten either lesson, and once in awhile I even remember to acknowledge them at a critical time. In the spring of 1988, for instance, an Oregon tom came trotting by because he thought the hen he heard earlier was moving away. In fact, I had called softly to make him think exactly that because he had been strutting just out of range and out of sight. The ploy worked beautifully, but when the Rio Grande gobbler committed himself to finding that hen he was moving too fast for a decent shot, and he was about to put some brush between us when I stopped him cold with a loud cluck from a mouth call. He was a beautiful, mature tom that weighed in the neighborhood of 19 pounds.

Back in the early days, when I simply wore blue jeans and a waist length camo poncho while turkey hunting, I often sat behind a bush that hid my pants and peered through it, and that's a very poor calling position. I still like some scattered cover between me and a turkey, even when I'm in full camo, but, like many experienced turkey hunters, I now prefer to sit with my back against a stout tree, preferably one with a trunk as wide or wider than my shoulders, whenever possible. Not only can you sit still longer with a good back rest, but your view on most sides is clearer, and you can point your shotgun freely in a wider arc. which is important when a tom doesn't come straight to you on the route you expect him to take. For reasons that will be explored further in another chapter this is also the safest position for you to call from.

Even though you might feel exposed, sitting in front of a tree or a stump, you won't be noticed IF you can remain still and if you're dressed in clothing that helps blur your form. Point your shotgun in the direction you expect the tom to come from and if you can prop it up with your elbows across your knees so much the better. Otherwise, don't raise the gun or put a hand operated call down while a tom is in view until you see that his head is obscured by a fold of land, a tree, thick brush or his own tail feathers if he happens to be strutting and in range.

In turkey hunting even the simple act of sitting down, especially when it's dark, takes some thought. If it's warm there's always the chance you'll sit too close to a rattlesnake but that is extremely rare and can be avoided if you simply look around first. More likely, you'll sit on a ground hugging cactus like I did in New Mexico once, or be embraced by poison oak like California hunters often are.

A few years ago I had an interesting experience toward the end of the season here in California. I was after a frustrating old tom (at leastI like to think he was a longbeard) that always gobbled repeatedly at daybreak then walked away with who knows how many hens. I hoped to eventually bump into him when he was lonely but it didn't happen. Still, I kept trying and one morning I found myself listening to him leave the roost and join up with a hen or two, after which I figured he'd walk into a nearby basin, as usual, and disappear for the day.

This time I planned to keep track of him for awhile so I moved to the edge of the tree smothered basin and sat down with my back against a stout oak. I yelped loudly a few times with a raspy box, because it often gets a response when nothing else does, then settled in to wait. I hoped the tom would open up in a few minutes but he didn't utter a sound. Behind me, though, a turkey I didn't expect gobbled once and another tom yelped hoarsely. Gad, I thought, here they come. Right then I became aware of something biting my neck, and something else crawling around inside the face mask I happened to be wearing. I was covered with ants!

I rolled out from the tree and looked back toward where the gobble had come from. Three curious young toms strolled into view a few seconds later and I was empty handed. My box call was more than an arm's length away and my mouth calls were neatly tucked inside my daypack, even farther away than the box. Worse yet, my shotgun was next to the box call, and I couldn't reach it, either. I just laid there, trying to mimic a rock, while the ants did their thing, and just when I was about to start swatting, the toms turned around and went back. I slithered over to my gun and, still on my belly, clucked a

With his back against a stout pine Ed Sweet has a comfortable position from which to call. He also has room to shift when necessary or swing his shotgun barrel 180 degrees.

couple times with the box and set it aside again. Incredibly the turkeys came back again and when they were 20 yards away I shot what looked like the leader of the group, a 15 pound jake.

Although I wound up shooting from a prone position right then, I don't like to lie down and talk turkey under normal circumstances. You can hide that way but your field of view is restricted and you might as well forget it if an old tom comes in from behind, as they are apt to do at times. It is not a good idea to squat or sit on your knees, either. Both positions are tiring and it's impossible to concentrate fully on turkeys when your muscles are straining or your feet are numb.

Because of increased hunting pressure in the West there are places where the gobblers are definitely not easy to fool. When I have a choice I like to hunt in terrain where long range visibility is restricted and land contours are many. Toms in such terrain can be troublesome, true, but I think they tend to come closer naturally because they are used to hearing other turkeys that can't be seen readily. If you get between them and their hens, or if they are separated in the first place, the odds of luring in a lovelorn tom in such terrain are good, indeed.

The open ridges, mesas and plains present in many parts of the West create another set of headaches, especially when it comes to calling position. Although you can occasionally talk a tom in from 300 to 400 yards, don't bank on it. If there's any way in the world to get closer before getting serious, do it. Try to get within 150 yards of a tom on his roost or on the ground before calling but remember there is such a thing as too close. Somewhere there's a fine line. Step over it and you may be seen, and if not that, you might be heard.

I remember one morning in southern Oregon when I almost had it made, but not quite. After hearing two toms gobbling on a ridge in the ponderosa pines, I set up no more than 100 yards away to call to them from a little saddle that looked like a perfect place for them to display for my reluctant hen. The toms definitely listened to my coy hen yelps and one of them came close enough so I could hear him drum enticingly in between gobbles and just out of view. He seemed to tire of that, however, and when his buddy joined him both birds wandered on up the ridge.

I followed after them and when I stopped on the edge of an opening to yelp a couple times the answering gobble was as exciting as an earthquake. Ducking back from the open wooded flat I was approaching, I crouched next to a sturdy pine. All it took was a couple

This California turkey came within shotgun range even though John Higley was seated against the open trunk of an oak tree.

of yelps and the birds started coming back. The only problem was that I couldn't see clearly from my quickly chosen calling spot so I scrambled to another tree and started calling again. The silence was sudden, and total. But why? I believe now that the two Romeos heard something out of place. Sure, hens make noises, too, but probably nothing like a 200 pound snake slithering from one tree to the next on a bed of dry pine needles and oak leaves. Those turkeys did not make a peep for the rest of the day.

During the spring in New Mexico, Mike Ballew and I used binoculars to spot three nice Merriam's toms on a little green knob in the ponderosa pines half a mile away. Actually, a small herd of mule deer caught our eye first, then we noticed the toms strutting around among the deer. We figured, rightly, that there must be hens nearby, as well.

To get in close without spooking the deer, which would certainly scare the turkeys halfway to Colorado, we circled wide to put a juniper dotted finger ridge between us. From below we approached a dogleg corner of the ridge that the birds and deer were on. Finally, we sat down in a line of junipers just at the edge of the bend and beyond a saddle, where we now heard the turkeys feeding slowly downhill. Some coarse yelps, to duplicate the raspy sounds of one or two of the hens we heard, was all it took to convince a mature tom to come in and investigate, and Mike shot him at 21 yards.

In open terrain the turkeys gravitate to the sheltered breaks, which lead into river bottoms or canyons off the flats, and usually have more cover than surrounding areas. Often they pitch off a rim in the evening and sail into roost trees just below the lip or somewhere farther below. Here again, in order to set up in a spot that is a natural place for them to go, you need to know the lay of the land, and the routes the turkeys usually follow when they fly down from a particular roost site in the morning. Interestingly, many eastern turkeys roost over water, as did a fine tom I killed in Alabama a short time ago. Western toms don't seem to be water oriented that way, perhaps because there are few sloughs and most mountain streams are too noisy for their liking.

In some of the canyons I've hunted the turkeys habitually follow stock and game trails along the creeks and dry washes because those are the easiest routes to travel in rugged terrain. The right place to be at dawn might be along such a game trail, in an opening where the toms commonly go to strut, along a route through gentle terrain where the birds are used to fanning out to feed, or somewhere on the finger ridge they commonly use to leave a canyon and reach the flats above.

A decoy is helpful in open terrain at times but here again it's best not to try and make a tom cross too much open ground to get to it. As a lure, however, it's hard to beat a decoy set up in a spot where you know an incoming tom will see it. When his mind is on the plastic imitation he will be completely fooled for the time being and may even try to breed with the imposter. I've had toms come to decoys in the morning and evening and hens come to inspect them, too. Naturally, if there are any toms with the hens they'll be right there in front of you.

As I indicated earlier, decoys definitely do work at least part of the time and the only reason I don't use mine more often is because I like to travel light and don't want to carry it everywhere I go. Decoys are helpful at times, though, and you should consider having one as part of your arsenal, even if you don't use it very often. If I was hunting with a bow I'd use a decoy most of the time because the imposter would provide a range estimate to any tom that came close and it might also distract a tom's attention and allow me more time for a shot.

Turkey hunting is always interesting because you never quite know what's going to happen next. If you have the ability to adapt as you go along, though, you'll be surprised by what might work for you at times. For instance, it sometimes pays to have a plan-B up your sleeve when plan-A backfires like a downtown bus.

One spring morning I heard a tom gobbling in a favorite area, and I started hurrying toward him because he sounded hot, and I was sure I could call him in if I got into position quick enough. As I got closer, however, I realized a pattern was forming. The tom was not only moving in a straight line, he seemed to be gobbling with each and every step. I stopped in my tracks to listen more carefully because I suspected, correctly it turned out, that another hunter was reeling the bird in with the lure of hen talk I couldn't hear. A shot rang out just seconds later to confirm my suspicions.

Now I do not begrudge another hunter his turkey but an incident like that can ruin your whole day. As I trudged back up the hill I came down on, however, an idea crossed my mind. A few days before I'd heard a tom gobbling in another location a few miles away. The sun was climbing higher and my time was growing short, but I drove the paved back roads and reached the spot by 9 o'clock.

It was warm and I easily worked up a sweat on my fast paced hike along a brushy ridge. Soon I bailed off and dropped into a patch of black oaks and pines near where I suspected the other gobbler had been. I crawled up to the trunk of a live oak and propped myself up against it. In a few minutes I took out my box call and stroked the paddle a few times. Gobble-obble-obble!

Mike Ballew got this nice Merriam's tom in New Mexico after using land contours to move in close enough to call him in. Mike first saw the bird with binoculars a half mile away.

John Higley with a round tailed Rio Grande tom that came to a decoy in the open canyon country of northern California.

The turkeys obviously hadn't heard or seen me getting into position and to prove it they soon appeared in front of me about 25 yards away. The one with the longest beard, about 8 inches, went home with one tired, happy and lucky hunter. It was just a few minutes after 10 o'clock when I got back to my pickup.

That incident brings up the subject of competition among hunters. Throughout the West, including some increasingly rare spots in California, it is still possible to have a flock of turkeys to yourself, especially on a week day. That in itself is a luxury according to Ed Sweet, who was comparing his home state of Idaho with his former Pennsylvania stomping grounds.

"Back there you'll find a road practically every half mile," Ed remembered, "and you could bet that if you found a tom anywhere that 16 other hunters knew where he was, too. There were turkey hunters' vehicles parked at the end of every road. You really had to know your turkeys to get one in a situation like that. We may not have as many turkeys out here (Idaho) but there's a lot more land and there aren't as many hunters, either." Come to think of it that's not a bad trade off, and one of the best reasons for turkey hunting in the West.

Obviously, there's more to turkey hunting than simply being in the woods at the right time. The way you apply your hunting skills, and adapt to the various situations as they present themselves, will add or subtract greatly from your overall turkey hunting success.

Chapter 10

Locating Western Turkeys, Spring And Fall

It goes without saying that there's more to turkey hunting than the actual hunt. Serious hunters spend quite a bit of time searching out places to hunt long before entering the woods with a shotgun in hand. The search takes thought, conversation, review, foot work, and luck. Finding turkeys in the West can be a chore because there's so much ground to cover, but once you've got a good spot it may have turkeys year after year, and it will pay off more often as you learn the habits of the birds that occupy the area.

Realize, though, that just because you see turkeys while on a deer hunt somewhere in the fall does not mean that they will be in the same area come spring. They may be in the same drainage somewhere, true, but in the western mountains that can mean anywhere in several thousand acres.

While there are places in the West where the same roosts are used every month of the year, there are other areas where the birds migrate with the seasons. Referring to the situation in Idaho, Ed Sweet noted that both Merriam's and Rio Grandes might wind up in the same river bottom habitat come winter, and that the Merriam's usually start back up a mountain in the spring while the Rios basically stay put. Sometimes, as in the part of central Montana where I hunted with Rob Hazlewood in 1988, the birds have no place to go and must take whatever Mother Nature dishes out to them. Evidently, they are up to the challenge as turkeys are thick in the area.

In the oak dotted lowlands of California you might find turkeys in the same location practically anytime while in mountainous areas there's often some migratory movement and elevation change in both spring and fall.

While it's definitely fun to find turkeys anytime, spring hunters should remember that the distribution of the birds will change dramatically when fall flocks, which are intact all winter, finally break up. Suddenly, there will be a lot of roaming as the hens search for nesting areas and toms follow. At the same time dominance will be re-established and in the process some toms may roam far and wide looking for companionship. Young hens may also wander quite a bit before they find a place that suits them and normally a tom or two will be right with them. Eventually things will settle down and there will be groups of turkeys spread out in a general area rather than large flocks of birds in basically one location.

Because of the inevitable break up I personally like to wait until just prior to the spring season opener to locate the birds. The closer to opening day, the better, because then there's some guarantee that the birds will still be nearby when things get serious.

Although nothing is set in stone, it's generally true that if the turkeys are in a particular area one year they'll be back again the next. Variables aside, the older hens will often nest somewhere in one basic location year after year, and once again, where there are hens there will almost always be toms. That's a fairly safe bet.

As a rule of thumb, the deeper local hunters are into turkey hunting the more protective they become about their "secret" spots. This is as true in the West as anywhere and it's probably caused by a couple of factors. One, turkey hunting is usually a game best played in solitude, and two, it takes a lot of effort to locate the birds initially, especially on public ground. In the West, as elsewhere, a lot of the better turkey hunting is found on private land where permission to trespass is normally difficult to come by unless you happen to be a friend or relative of a landowner. So public land opportunities, while still increasing, are something of a secret between hunters.

Don't despair. Sometime in the past even the most experienced hunter had to find a place to hunt. In fact, when you do pin someone down after you've hunted turkeys for awhile, chances are good that you'll discover you've both been concentrating on the same general area all along. There are certainly some real secret spots left in the turkey hunter's world—but there aren't many of them!

Opening that first door is, of course, the toughest part. The logical place to start is with the state game departments, which are usually willing to assist hunters in locating broad basic areas, at least. An upland game specialist on the state or local level can give you some good advice and in cases where turkey hunters are limited by quota the printed regulations will actually direct you to the best turkey range.

There are other people to talk to, as well. Local sporting goods dealers in or near areas where turkeys are hunted are a good choice. If they carry a good selection of turkey calls and paraphernalia they should have some advice for aspiring hunters, especially if they want their return business. In some areas the local chapter of the National Wild Turkey Federation (based in Edgefield, South Carolina), a turkey call manufacturer, sports show, or a sporting goods outlet will sponsor a turkey hunting seminar prior to the spring season, and while such an event is usually fun for all who attend, it is especially helpful for newcomers to the sport.

Looking for tracks is a big part of scouting for turkeys anywhere. Any sandy, muddy or dusty spot may have turkey tracks like this if the birds are in the area.

Don't hesitate to talk with local residents as you canvass potential turkey hunting areas. More than one guy pumping gas has offered vital tips to hunters in the past and sometimes a friendly private landowner has some interesting things to say. My friend Terry Knight, outdoor writer and avid California turkey hunter, has had good success locating turkeys around reservoirs where hunting is permitted by asking the bass fishermen. They are often out early and fishing quietly when they hear a gobbler sound off on a nearby ridge. Terry tells me that female employees of local stores have also been helpful in the check out line. Regardless, by combining bits and pieces of information you should gradually get closer to homing in on actual hunting spots.

There's a lot to be said for listening, too. My family moved to northern California early one spring in the mid-1970's from the southern part of the state, and while I knew there were turkeys close to my new home, I didn't know where they were and I was prepared to sit the season out while we got settled. However, since I'd already been hunting turkeys for several years, any mention of the birds naturally got my attention.

Ordinarily I don't eavesdrop, but one afternoon, when I walked out of the local barber shop, I almost bumped into two guys talking and one of them was saying something about seeing turkeys. My ears perked up and I heard the name of a road mentioned. The season had just opened a few days before but we were still unpacking and I really didn't intend to hunt—until that instant.

A couple of days later I drove along that road in bright sunlight just to check things out. Oh, I did have a shotgun, a turkey call, and some camouflage clothes along but I assure you I really didn't expect to put them to use.

I still wonder if I'll ever be as lucky again. I stopped right on the road next to a woods bordered meadow, stood next to my pickup, and made a few yelps with a box call, whereby a gobbler replied immediately from somewhere in the trees on the far side of the meadow. I found a better place to park, dug out the shotgun, donned a camo shirt, hat and headnet, and hurried toward the spot. Within 20 minutes I called two toms up to 15 yards and got a dandy adult bird to take home with me. That's about as good as it gets in a new area on the first time out.

The first thing I did when I overheard those guys outside the barber shop was find the road they mentioned on a county road map. New areas, even now, are often located initially on road maps, USDA

Forest Service, or Bureau of Land Management maps. Then I like to get a feel for the lay of the land by studying topographic maps that show contours.

Map reading can save a lot of steps in the field. My friend Cliff Dewell, an avid turkey hunter from northern California, recently pointed to a spot on a topo map and said, "There's got to be turkeys right there."

Cliff had never been to that particular location but he knew there were turkeys a ridge or two away and he knew what type of terrain and elevation he was looking for, namely a series of basins near the headwaters of a creek, below 4,000 feet. Hiking into the area a few days later he did find turkeys, as expected.

Once you figure out where some turkeys might be you have to get out in the field and find them and you do that by sight, sound or sign, or a combination of the three. Looking for sign is probably the surest method and the one I rely on most, although I always enjoy hearing and seeing turkeys and I'm ever alert for either possibility.

Turkeys leave six basic physical signs of their presence: tracks, droppings, feathers, scratchings, dusting spots and during the spring, wing-tip strut marks. Of these, tracks are what you'll most likely find

These tracks in the mud are between 4-1/2 and 4-3/4 inches long, meaning they were left by a tom. Hen tracks are a full inch shorter.

93

Montana hunter Rob Hazlewood closely inspects a back road for any sign of turkeys.

One good place to find sign is around a water source, either a stream or a pond like this one in southern Oregon.

because, in theory, turkeys have to leave them everywhere they go. That is not always the case, however, because they don't leave many tracks on hard ground during a dry spring.

I look for tracks by driving or walking dirt roads and hiking game trails. Once, after a futile morning long search, I found a turkey track on a fresh gopher mound. More likely you'll spot them in the dust, mud, sand or snow somewhere. A fresh, complete track in front of my nose makes me grin like a fool, and once a partial toe print in a small smudge of mud on an unused road led to the discovery of a spot that held turkeys all season long.

There are variations in everything concerning turkeys but you can usually tell the difference between clear adult hen and tom tracks by measuring them. Allan Jeffers, a California taxidermist specializing in turkeys, says the tracks of mature toms average out at 4-1/2 inches from the tip of the center toe, not including the toenail, to the heel. Hen tracks are an inch shorter as a rule. I measure tracks wherever I find them and my figures coincide with Allan's.

Droppings are another sure sign of turkeys being in the neighborhood and they can outlast tracks because rain is less likely to

Turkey droppings are round or somewhat "j" shaped. Size and configuration varies but generally the j droppings are made by toms.

wash them away. However, there obviously aren't as many droppings as tracks and you'll find most of them on pine needle rugs or dirt roads where there isn't a lot of vegetation to obscure them. Hens normally deposit wads about the circumference of quarters but toms, so the theory goes, leave droppings in the shape of an abbreviated "j". Actually, size is probably more important than shape which may be regulated somewhat by diet. The bigger droppings in any configuration spell tom to me. Fresh droppings are green with a splash of white and the freshest are still soft. Older sign may be almost black and shriveled but sometimes a little white will still show.

Droppings are also associated with roost trees. Such trees aren't easy to find initially, but they are worth keeping an eye out for anytime you cut cross country during a scouting trip. Depending on the location, western turkeys might roost in ponderosa pines, digger

A large dropping like this is definite sign that turkeys are in an area.

Depending on the location western turkeys may roost in large digger pines like this, ponderosa pines, oaks of one kind or another and cottonwood trees to name a few favorites.

John Higley inspects a typical turkey scratch in a bed of leaves.

pines, cottonwood trees, and oaks of one kind or another. Look for trees with branches at least a couple inches in diameter and stout enough to hold a turkey with enough space between limbs to let a turkey fly in and out freely.

Roost trees are usually located off the side of ridges, along wooded draws in the bottom of a canyon, or in the riparian habitat near a stream. I've seen turkeys pitch off a rugged canyonside and sail a half mile to roosts in the bottom, and I've seen them fly a few yards from a flat to pines on the sidehill below. Contoured terrain is generally the rule, although turkeys are certainly able to fly directly up into a roost tree on the flats if the need arises. Regardless, a regularly used roost will have lots of droppings on the ground beneath it but you'll have to look very carefully to find the sign around a seldom used tree.

As turkeys go about the business of being turkeys they often leave scratchings as they rake through leaves and pine needles looking for seeds, grubs, beetles, acorns and other tidbits. Sometimes a flock really works a spot over, other times you may find only one or two wash pan size bare spots where the duff has been scraped away. In ranch and farm country piles of cow dung may be turned over or scratched apart by turkeys, as well as other critters, looking for the insects that hide in or under them or the grain the cow didn't digest.

While we're still on the subject of physical signs I'll mention dropped feathers. Actually, I find a lot more tracks and droppings than feathers but every once in awhile a wing or breast feather turns up, and occasionally a pile of them tells me where some other predator had supper. I'm sure more feathers are shed during the fall

Feathers, too, tell a story. The black tipped feather in this photo is from the body of a tom; the buff tipped feather is from a hen.

moult than any other time. However, it's reasonable to assume that toms dislodge a few feathers during spring jousts so feathers are worth looking for like everything else.

A year ago a friend of mine scouted long and hard one day in a favorite area and the only sign he found was one solitary black tipped breast feather from a tom. He was discouraged because he expected to see tracks all over the place and didn't. When the season opened, though, he heard toms in several directions, and one day during the first week he actually saw 17 toms in the same roost area! It doesn't take much sign to tell you the turkeys are HERE!

I can't picture a time when strut marks would be more evident than other turkey sign but finding the grooves cut by a tom's wing tips as he pirouettes around on a patch of dirt somewhere will definitely send a tingle up a turkey hunter's spine, even if you're standing among a dozen tracks. As the season approaches strut marks may also mark a strutting site, a place regularly used by the toms to show off, and sometimes a good place to set up and call.

Dusting spots are the last sign to be mentioned and probably the least important for spring scouting unless the ground is already summer dry and there is loose soil available. Like other birds, turkeys take dust baths to help rid themselves of parasites, and while they are usually few and far between, the depressions they leave are quite noticeable on open banks, old roads and similar spots.

Obviously, you can look for sign anytime during the day. If you're ambitious you can get out before daybreak and locate turkeys by sound much as you would during the season. Otherwise, listen for them in late afternoon right up until dark because the toms commonly gobble just before and just after they fly up for the night. Don't forget to listen for any kind of turkey sounds no matter when you scout, however.

You might also use a call like a hen during the day to start a turkey gobbling and thus locate the birds prior to a hunt. If nothing else you'll have a chance to practice under field conditions and your calls will sound different outside in the woods than they do at home.

However, where a pre-season answer or two is quite enough for some hunters, others like to try calling gobblers in, if they can, just to watch them or take photographs. Heck, I enjoy that myself, but I really don't think it's a good idea to fool with the same birds very often. One friend of mine recently complained that the toms on the ranch he was hunting almost never came into shotgun range after opening day like they did prior to the season. Could it be that he

Once in awhile youll locate strut marks, made by a toms wingtips as they drag the ground. They are a definite sign of breeding activity in an area.

Another physical sign of turkeys are dusting spots like this one made in ashes where a slash pile was burned.

created a bunch of call shy gobblers by toying with them too often? Quite likely, I think.

The last way to find turkeys on their home ground is by sight. A lot of western turkey country is open enough to use binoculars effectively and I almost always scout with a pair of them handy to check out questionable dark spots in the distance, or to locate and watch turkeys that I hear somewhere. It's always fun to see the birds you'll soon be hunting, and even if you don't spot turkeys right away there's always lots of other wildlife to see in any good turkey range. I don't know about you but as a hunter I never get tired of watching deer, elk, squirrels, coyotes, hawks and any other critters you might see on a typical scouting trip.

Finding turkeys in the spring is one thing, in the fall it's another. When most fall seasons open the birds are pretty well grouped to-gether, meaning that you might have to cover much more country because they obviously can't be everywhere at once. Generally, the hens and poults will be together in large bunches and the toms will roam in bachelor groups, although all the birds may be in the same general area due to the food supply or some other element that brings them together.

Regardless, fall flocks are never as vocal as turkeys are in the spring. You may hear some toms sound off once in awhile, but don't bank on it. More than likely all you'll hear is "flock talk" meaning muted clucks, purrs and yelps as the turkeys keep track of one another. There will be more talk between them just off the roost as, indeed, there is with other upland game birds such as quail. I've located fall flocks successfully later in the day by hiking along the ridges and calling often, then listening very carefully for any kind of turkey sounds in reply.

A cluck or a few yelps from real turkeys are all it takes to make a fine fall day even brighter.

This hunter uses a map to help pinpoint possible turkey hunting hotspots.

– Chapter 11 –

The Fall Difference

While the search for basic turkey signs goes on in the fall actually pinpointing a flock is often a matter of listening, like it is in the spring, even though the birds are less vocal as a rule.

I remember a long morning in northern California many years ago. For several hours I walked across the broad, rocky plain, following the snake-like route of a spotty creek in the canyon below. Time after time I paused to yelp loudly with a mouth call or box, and time after time I was greeted only by the sound of the southern breeze, forerunner of afternoon rain. It was the middle of November, fall turkey season was open, the birds were grouped together, and so far I hadn't a clue as to where.

I was not surprised. Although fall flocks do circulate around the same habitual roost sites at times, the area I was in had potential roost trees, mainly digger pines, in every little basin along the stream for at least 10 miles. The birds were prone to roam and that's exactly what they did. I smiled to myself as I hiked along and wondered if I was, indeed, having fun yet.

It was just about noon when I sent another series of yelps off the flat into a notch in the canyon wall as I had 50 times before. But this time there was something different about the echo and I realized that a genuine turkey hen or two had yelped back even before the sounds of my calls died away. I yelped some more and the unseen turkeys repeated themselves. Finally I've found them, I thought, and then uncertainty crept into my mind. What do I do now?

Although turkeys can occasionally be called in the fall, much as they are in the spring, the best odds of luring them conventionally occur early in the day when the birds are regrouping after a long night on the roost. In this case, the flock had already been together for hours and I doubted that they would ever respond to my calls with any more enthusiasm than they had. Somehow I would have to create an edge.

Because turkeys really like company (there's safety in numbers`

Hunting conditions are different in the fall but hunters who make the effort can still take turkeys like this nice tom.

and because the leaders of a fall flock will only rarely come in to inspect a strange turkey (perhaps you) one proven tactic used by those who wish to enjoy a fall calling experience involves breaking up a flock then calling individual members back. This is not too difficult to do when you manage to separate hens and poults because they will start trying to regroup before long much like scattered quail.

The tough part is dividing the flock in the first place. If you simply scare them away as a unit they won't have any reason to return. I've read many times that the best way to confuse flock members is to rush the birds while yelling and generally raising cain. However, I've also been in spots where rushing was impossible unless you could fly off a cliff or didn't mind breaking a leg.

If you do manage to pull it off the idea is to set-up right where you got into the flock then yelp like an old hen or kee-kee like a poult and watch sharply for a bird or two to sneak back in. It works like a charm if you can remain still and not be seen, and since both sexes are generally fair game in the fall the first bird that shows up can be dinner shortly thereafter.

Of course, hens and poults aren't going to be as large as mature toms, and some may not think hunting them is quite as rewarding as hunting gobblers no matter what time of year it is. I suppose that has something to do with the effort you put into a hunt or a personal conviction that hens shouldn't be taken at any time. From the perspective of a California hunter I would argue that point simply because in this state, with the most liberal fall bag limit (would you believe it's one turkey per day?), and a spring limit of two bearded turkeys, the estimated population has grown from 15,000 to 100,000 in the last few years. Some hunting pressure is actually good for wild turkeys as long as it isn't applied during critical periods. With the exception of wild pheasants in some areas, all upland game birds are subject to either-sex hunting and they withstand it very well.

The first fall turkey I ever shot was a nice tom from a group of, maybe, 10 birds that I didn't call in. Instead, I followed several turkeys for hours by listening to them talk back and forth, mainly a cluck here and a cluck there, and occasionally I prompted them to yelp back by calling to them myself. Because of the terrain, which was difficult enough to get around in when I wasn't hurrying, I never could rush the birds but when they started feeding up a draw toward the top of a rise I had time to circle around them and come down from above.

In a few minutes I was in the middle of them, and while I didn't think about it, I had two ways to go and I chose the easy way out. The birds were scattering all around me.

Some flew out over the hillside toward the flats below, at least one circled all the way around me in the air only 15 yards away, one landed in a nearby pine tree and the tom I shot rushed uphill right into my lap. It was mass confusion for about 10 seconds and it paid off.

Afterwards it dawned on me that it would have been more fun to call a bird in but the idea of it didn't dampen my pleasure at that moment by any means. Later, I learned that it's not unusual at all for flushing turkeys to go in every direction, including right toward the hunter who's scaring them.

Some of the most successful fall hunters I know actually use bird dogs, retrievers mainly, to sniff out the quiet flocks and break them up. Then the turkeys can either be shot on the wing or called in, if the dog will lie down quietly that is. I do not like to shoot turkeys on the fly, personally, but I have done it successfully as a last resort, at the end of a long hunt. Incidentally, before taking old Rover afield make sure hunting fall turkeys with dogs is legal in your state.

As in the spring, tracks can lead you to fall turkeys. This is a hen track about 3-1/2 inches long.

Separation is generally the key to fall calling, especially in the case of hens and poults. Small bands of older toms may be difficult to call even if you do break them up because they're naturally more wary and less excited about being apart. Give them some extra time, then call simply with clucks, yelps and even kee-kee's from the spot where you separated them, and listen very carefully for any sort of reply.

Although I haven't tried it I've heard of hunters scaring fall toms to separate them just prior to, and even after, going to roost. The idea is that the toms will be more anxious than ever to find each other come daybreak. In California that doesn't work very well because in the fall shooting hours begin at 8 o'clock in the morning and the birds are down on the ground earlier than that. Then it's up to you to divide the birds somehow and get between them to call later in the day.

I do not like to shoot a turkey on the wing but it is possible and does happen, especially in the fall when you bump into a flock by accident or design.

A typical fall group of hens and rapidly maturing poults.

Sometimes you get unexpected help—that is, it's help if you recognize it as such. One morning, for instance, my son Mark and I watched two toms fly off the roost at the same time, and while they even gobbled once or twice when we called, they were only interested only in having breakfast together. We were on a slope above the turkeys playing a one sided game of tag with them, and not getting anywhere, when we accidently bumped into a couple of blacktail deer which immediately bounced down the slope right past the turkeys, neatly pushing them in two different directions.

Later Mark called one of the toms back and anchored the 17 pounder with a 2-3/4 inch magnum load of No.6 shot.

Turkey hunting in the fall is different. For one thing you have to work harder to find the quiet birds. You have to endure some awful weather at times, and learn a different calling routine. However, you also have less competition.

Fact is, turkeys are easier to find when they're vocal in the spring than they are in the fall when they're quiet and banded together, whether in small or large groups. The extra difficulty discourages some hunters at the outset, but more than that there's almost too much going on in the fall for western hunters to go overboard on turkeys at that time.

In the states that hold fall turkey hunts—and not all of them do—the season normally opens in November, a time when late deer and elk seasons are still going on, bear hunting is in full swing, the geese and ducks are showing up in your favorite marsh, and other upland game from squirrels to pheasants are fair game. More than that, there are even places on the West Coast where the steelhead and salmon are running. It is hard for a sportsman to know where to turn and few are willing to devote the time necessary to become really proficient fall turkey hunters.

Fall sport will increase in popularity as interest in turkeys grows throughout the West but I doubt that it will ever have the mass appeal of the spring season. That is not to say it isn't fun. In fact, for the harried spring hunter, who feels there's too much competition in the areas he frequents, fall hunting may just be the answer to his prayers.

Chapter 12

Bowhunting For Turkeys

It seems reasonable, given the increasing popularity of turkey hunting these days, that some successful hunters would find shotgunning too easy and take to the field, at least part of the time, with bow and arrow instead. Always ready for a challenge, bowhunters have picked a winner in wild turkeys. It's not impossible to bag a gobbler with a string gun, but it isn't easy, either.

Cliff Dewell, who has been mentioned before, is an incredibly successful bowhunter with wide experience in the West and at least one trip to Africa under his belt. He regularly takes elk and deer with his archery gear but if you asked him I think he'd say bagging a sharp eyed gobbler is one of the toughest tricks of all.

Consider the problems. Turkeys have exceptional eyesight and good hearing. They can see you move when you don't think you have and they hear the brush scratch your clothes if you have to turn for a better view. They are also quick and a bowhunter who is spotted before he has his bow at full draw might as well just wave good-by because he isn't going to get that bird.

What you need, then, is a turkey that comes in to your call, gets close enough for a realistic shot, and has his vision obstructed temporarily at just the right time for you to come to full draw. Then, of course, you have to shoot straight and hit your target in a vital spot. Overall the chances of everything coming together are about as good as finding steak at a health food store.

Under his feathers an average tom will measure only 12 inches from the base of his neck to the bottom of his breast. The vital heart and lungs are located forward of the intestines and don't take up much more room than a doubled fist. Miss the vitals, or fail to break the backbone, and you could have a real chase on your hands.

A shotgunner can easily aim for the head and neck, knowing that a few pellets there will result in a clean kill most every time. A bowhunter who hits a tom in the neck was most likely aiming for

Idaho hunter Ed Sweet likes bowhunting and shotgunning. Here he hefts a nice tom he took with a bow.

another spot and made a lucky hit. With an arrow you have to be more selective as to angle, range, and position.

Idaho turkey hunter Ed Sweet has taken several turkeys with the bow, including a nice bird with a 9-1/2 inch beard in 1987, and he's passed many up without shooting even at very close range.

"Sometimes you just can't get the right angle on them," Ed said recently, "even when they're just 15 yards away. I try not to take what I consider to be questionable shots at any range."

That takes will power, obviously, and Ed evidently has it because he's hunted turkeys for so long and he doesn't feel the need to prove anything to anyone by taking what he considers an unnecessary chance. Still, Ed admits that his self-imposed range limitation (he hates to shoot at a tom more than 20 yards away) may be short for some hunters who are capable of pin-point accuracy out to 30 yards or so. It is interesting to note that Cliff Dewell doesn't care to shoot long, either, and for that reason he normally passes on several apparently good opportunities every season before finally letting an arrow fly.

So where do you aim on a turkey? Both hunters said the best shot is from the side and the leading edge of the wing or "shoulder" is where they aim. An angling shot that you know would pierce the vitals will also work but head on and strutting shots are usually not taken because mostly what you're seeing is feathers and if you don't hit dead center the bird will get away—or try to anyway.

Bowhunters, of course, use the same kind of turkey calls shotgunners use. However, the advantage of diaphragm calls is apparent when a tom is getting close and you want to be not only seductive but ready to shoot. You can cluck or yelp lightly to lure the tom the last few yards without ever moving your hands, if you can use a mouth call.

Even more important than call choice, though, is calling position. Years ago I saw Cliff Dewell set up between two bushes with a shooting lane in front but both he and Ed Sweet are more apt to station themselves on the edge of an opening with a large tree trunk at their back and a scattering of trees or other obstructions in front. A roll of land directly in front is always good since a turkey will probably be in range already when he walks into view.

Ed likes to sit on his knees (this was mentioned before and not recommended because your legs might fall asleep when the circulation is cut off) and while he does experience some discomfort at times he thinks the trade off is worth the mobility possible from such a stance.

The hardest part of bowhunting for turkeys is coming to full draw once you call a tom into range.

"Sitting is most comfortable but a bowhunter needs to be able to pivot freely and you can't do that with your rear on the ground," Ed said. (One hunter I know solves the problem with a small, light-weight folding stool).

114

Sweet also emphasizes the importance of having some obstructions scattered between you and an incoming turkey because, "If you don't make sure there are things for the tom to walk behind that will block his view you'll never be able to draw on him successfully."

Both Dewell and Sweet like to use wide, sharp broadheads on turkeys and Ed adds finger-like grabbers behind the head so the arrow doesn't just "blow through" a bird without tearing at anything. Many turkeys are killed in their tracks with arrows but some that aren't hit right the first time (and you won't get a second chance) take off running or flying and it can take hours of searching to find them. Typical small game heads like blunts are simply not what turkey hunting calls for.

A turkey that dies instantly is no problem but one that flies or runs after a hit might ruin your whole day. To minimize the possibility of loss don't throw up your hands in despair when a tom takes off. Rather, stay aware of the things going on as the bird tries to escape. Did it fly off a ridge into a basin? Could you see it come down? Did you mark the spot? Did you lose sight of it, and if so did you hear it crash into branches or brush? Can you hear its final flops on the forest floor somewhere?

Even if the bird does seem to get away try following it from its last known position. Turkeys usually don't leave a blood trail, especially if they fly off, but you owe it to yourself and any game to make a real attempt at recovery if you suspect that it is, indeed, wounded.

Consider a feat Cliff Dewell pulled off a few years ago. To begin with the tom came in just like he was supposed to and he even posed long enough for Cliff to shoot. Unfortunately, the arrow was low and Cliff thought he just missed when the gobbler took off like a flushing quail. There was a skiff of fresh snow on the ground but no sign of a hit.

"He seemed fine," Cliff remembers," but I had a nagging feeling. I looked at the arrow and it was clean but when the tom jumped it didn't look quite right. I was able to see the bird sail into a basin so I followed after it."

An hour later Cliff actually jumped the turkey, which had been hiding in the brush. The bird, obviously weak, flew only a short distance and landed again. Meanwhile, Dewell discovered blood where the tom had been hiding. A friend joined Cliff and working together they found a few spots of blood in the snowy draw. An hour later they located the turkey again. This time the tom was too weak to fly and the hunters finally tackled it and put it out of its misery. Dewell's

California bowhunter Cliff Dewell likes to use a diaphragm call when a tom is moving in so he has his hands free.

arrow had just nicked one leg. The bird was fully 600 yards from where it was shot when the hunt was finally over.

"I still think about that one," Cliff admitted." It tripled my conviction that you've always got to follow up on a shot. The thought of possibly losing wounded game haunts me."

Smartly, some bowhunters now use tracking devices on turkeys. The trackers attach to any bow and carry nearly a quarter mile of light, strong nylon string, which is tied to the arrow where the point joins the shaft. Theoretically, even if you shoot through a turkey the arrow and string will go with it, allowing easier recovery if the bird flies or runs away. However, you have to be set up in the right place to use a tracker effectively. If there's too much brush the string might get caught and cause misery either before or after you shoot.

Obviously, camouflage is even more important for a bowhunter than someone with a shotgun. Both your bow and arrows should have a dull finish and you should be as invisible as possible, too. One thing to watch, however, is how you cover your face. I know a guy who missed a chance at a turkey when his head net pulled across his master eye when he anchored his hand against his cheek. With camo cream or a net held in place by elastic that kind of thing won't happen.

As for bows, while there seems to be some movement back to plain recurves, most hunters do choose compound bows for hunting. The obvious advantage is the let off of a compound, which allows you to draw and hold your position for nearly a minute before your arms feel like they're going to break off.

All things considered, hunting turkeys with bow and arrow is one of the most difficult pastimes in the hunter's world. Happily, it's not entirely impossible, because any ray of hope is what keeps the bowhunters coming back for more.

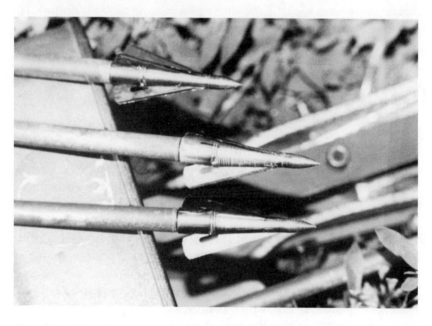

Sharp broadheads are a must for wild turkey hunting.

Chapter 13

Safety and Ethics

By its very nature you might suspect that hunting is a dangerous pastime. In reality, there are some accidents every year, but surprisingly few considering the number of hunters afield with rifles or shotguns in their hands.

Any accident, of course, is one too many, and as turkey hunting has grown in popularity during the last few years the number of reported accidents has increased along with hunting pressure. Some fatalities occur each year along with numerous non-fatal woundings with various degrees of severity. In addition, there are many close calls, and no doubt some minor injuries, that go unreported.

As you might suspect most of the accidents take place in the most heavily hunted states like Missouri, Alabama and New York (as reported in "Guide To The American Wild Turkey" published by the National Wild Turkey Federation, Inc., in 1986). The same book listed no turkey hunting related accidents in the West but I know of at least four in California and one in Oregon since then. One of the California accidents involved a friend of mine who was shot in the back and nearly killed one fall by another hunter who heard turkey sounds and saw unidentified movement.

Another accident involved world class bicycle racer Greg LeMond who was mistaken for a tom turkey and badly wounded during California's 1987 spring season when he was shot by a companion from about 50 yards away. LeMond has since recovered but his experience should be a warning to all of us. We aren't immune to the hazards and as hunter numbers increase throughout the West, the potential for more accidents grows with each season.

Because there isn't as much competition in the West as in the East or Midwest you are not as apt to encounter other hunters in your spot for the day, but that does not mean that you shouldn't be careful. I've been stalked by other hunters who heard me calling, and while I saw them coming and said something to identify myself, it still gave me an uneasy feeling.

Because you try to sound like a turkey, especially in the spring, and because you don't wear hunter orange or another bright color while hunting, it's realistic to think that a hunter who hears but does not see you might think you really are a turkey. That's all right if he only talks back to you and tries to lure you to him, which happens all the time, but if he tries to stalk you things get creepy in a hurry. During the spring of 1990 a friend of mine looked up from his calling in the Black Hills of Wyoming and saw another hunter pointing a scoped rifle at him from less than 100 yards. It did not sit well with my friend even though turkey hunting with a rifle is allowed in the area.

To minimize your chances of being mistaken for a turkey the National Wild Turkey Federation, Inc., has developed the following guidelines for defensive turkey hunting which are worth memorizing.

1. Never stalk a turkey. The chances of getting close enough for a shot are slim, but the chances of becoming involved in an accident are increased.

2. Eliminate the colors red, white and blue from your turkey hunting outfit. Red is the color most hunters count on to differentiate a gobbler's head from the hen's blue colored head. White can look like the snowball colored top of a gobbler's head. Wear something other than white tee shirts and socks, which can put you in danger and be seen by turkeys, as well.

3. Never move, wave or make turkey sounds to alert another hunter of your presence. A quick movement may draw fire. Yell in a loud voice and remain hidden.

4. Never attempt to approach closer than 100 yards to a roosting turkey.

5. Be particularly careful when using the gobbler call. The sound and motion may attract other hunters.

6. When selecting your calling position, don't try to hide so well that you cannot see what's happening around you.

119

7. Select a calling position that provides a background as wide as your shoulders, and one that will completely protect you from the top of your head down. Small trees won't hide slight movements of your hands and shoulders which might look like a turkey to another hunter who might be stalking your calls.

8. Camouflage conceals you. It does not make you invisible. When turkey hunting, think and act defensively. Remember, you are visible to both turkeys and hunters when you move even slightly.

9. Never shoot at a sound or movement.

10. When turkey hunting, assume that every sound you hear is made by another hunter.

The more I read over these rules the more sense they make. They point to the fact that if we all made sure of our target(s) before we shot most turkey hunting accidents would never happen. Regardless, of what you wear, how you sound, where you hide, or how you move, you shouldn't be mistaken for a turkey but......

Ironically, veteran turkey hunters often feel they are immune to accidents and yet studies show the average turkey hunting experience of most hunters who have made mistakes is 14 years.

There is one aspect of safety that hasn't been touched upon as yet and that is that you may very well be your own worst enemy if your gun handling practices are sloppy. I remember guiding one hunter who simply leaned his loaded shotgun against the fences we were about to climb or crawl through, until I had words with him. Of course, I always grabbed the gun and held it until he was on the other side, then I handed it over the top. When crossing a fence alone I place my gun on the ground on the other side of the barrier and point it in a safe direction without a shell in the chamber. After I get over I retrieve it but never barrel first.

Naturally, you will have a shell in the chamber anytime you're talking to a turkey because you won't want to make noise by injecting a round when a tom can hear you. But I like to think that I'm smart enough to remove the shell, temporarily at least, when I'm negotiating steep or rough terrain, or when I stop for a rest and want to prop the gun against a tree trunk rather than laying it down in wet grass or something. It should go without saying that anytime you're with someone else their safety should be your primary concern. Whether your shotgun is loaded or not, you never let the barrel point at a companion. Period.

No, turkey hunting is not a terribly dangerous pastime, especially in the West, but a little common sense can make it even safer for you and those around you.

There's another facet of turkey hunting that seems to go hand in hand with safety. That's the ethics of the sport. We are largely responsible for our own ethics, of course, the presence or lack of which is reflected in the way we treat our fellow hunters and the way we approach turkey hunting to begin with.

One offense that normally causes the hackles to rise on any sports minded hunter, is roost shooting. That is, shooting a tom out of a tree before daybreak. Legal shooting hours are usually set to guarantee the birds time to fly down but there are some greedy types who don't care how they get "their" turkey just as long as they have something to show off. There are also individuals who aren't satisfied with the legal limit and they may shoot several turkeys out of the same roost tree or simply keep hunting long after their bird(s) are in the freezer. I liken these types to any predators of society who run rough shod over the rules of common decency in any walk of life.

It's always important, from the aspect of safety as well as ethics, to try and determine if there are any other hunters in the spot you're hunting on a particular day. If you see another vehicle parked nearby you've got to assume you have company somewhere, and it behooves you to try to determine if another hunter is working on any gobbler that you hear before you make another move. You won't make any friends if you bust in on the gobbler another man happens to be calling.

Nor will you make a good impression by trespassing on private land without permission. Look-over-your-shoulder turkey hunting isn't enjoyable in the first place, and honest hunters should realize that entering the wrong areas out of desperation gives us all a bad name Come to think of it, so does littering on public or private land. It simply doesn't make sense to leave junk of any kind behind no matter where you happen to be.

Turkey hunters, in fact hunters in general, should be as close knit as a fraternity. Those who take unfair advantage of any game, who hunt to kill something without regard to fair chase, and those who annoy others in the field, and have a "bleep-you" attitude toward their fellow hunters, are only feeding the large propaganda mill that is behind the movement to ban hunting altogether. I think that what makes me angriest is knowing that some hunters, and I use the word loosely, simply don't give a dam about the consequences of their actions; their effect on others and the sport itself.

Preaching aside, let me say that I know no one's perfect all the time. The important thing is that we try to be fair to the game and considerate of others. Happily, most strangers I've met in the turkey woods, and most companions I've hunted with, seem to realize that turkey hunting, and any hunting for that matter, is a privilege and a way of life worth respecting and protecting. I only wish everyone felt the same way.

Chapter 14

State By State Review

This chapter begins a series on various turkey hunting regions in the West which will cover, in order, the Pacific States, Mountain States and the Southwest. Starting in the far west, this section will first take a look at turkey hunting in California, Oregon and Washington.

PACIFIC STATES

Wildlife biologist Harold Harper, now retired, was in on the ground floor of **California's** modern wild turkey program. At one time Harper told me he thought there was 16,000 square miles of potential turkey habitat in the state. That all of it may be populated sometime in the near future is certainly not an unpleasant thought.

As Harper said recently, "It doesn't surprise me anymore to hear about the new places where turkeys are suddenly being discovered, or where they'll turn up in another season or two."

Currently, there's more turkey hunting activity in California than any other state in the West. Thousands of hunters are out during the five week spring season and many of them try again in the fall when the season is normally open for a month. Both the seasons and the bag limits are generous. Hunters are allowed two bearded turkeys in the spring (although only one can be taken on a given day) and one wild turkey PER DAY in the fall.

In the years since the resurgence of the wild turkey program in the Golden State, in the early 1960's, huntable populations of turkeys have been established in at least 45 California counties. In the northern part of the state you can find birds in Shasta, Tehama, Siskiyou, Mendocino, Humboldt, Trinity and perhaps Lassen counties, to name a few. Bordering the inland valleys there's El Dorado, Yuba, Butte, Calaveras, Nevada, Placer and Amador counties. San Luis Obispo, Monterey and Sonoma counties have birds in the Coast Range, and there's more. I recently heard of birds being taken as far south as Kern, Tulare and San Bernardino counties and in 1994 San Diego County was open to turkey hunting for the first time.

This is not to say that all you have to do is jump in your car and go. As in many other states, California's wild turkeys got their initial foothold on private land because the habitat was right and there was an extra degree of protection from poaching. Some of the best hunting is still on such land where you naturally have to have permission to hunt or pay for the privilege through a lease agreement or by hiring a guide.

Happily, turkeys have increased in number and some have moved by themselves to adjacent public lands, while still others have been transplanted to such places by the California Department of Fish and Game (DFG). So the future seems bright. Already it's possible to find turkeys in such places as the Sequoia, Sierra, Stanislaus, El Dorado, Plumas, Tahoe, Los Padres, Mendocino, and Shasta-Trinity national forests. There are also birds on some DFG wildlife areas like Tehama and Spenceville, on scattered parcels of land managed by the Bureau of Land Management, and on some public land adjacent to foothills reservoirs like Shasta Lake, New Melones Lake and Lake Oroville. Timber company holdings and public utilities property open to the public sometimes have scattered populations and there is turkey hunting on a couple of military reservations in the Coastal Mountains.

You may find areas with turkeys from near sea level to 4,000 feet elevation and recently I found a track during the summer at almost 6,000 feet elevation. As for the type of turkey(s) found in this state both Merriam's and Rio Grandes were planted in various areas, along with early introductions of game farm raised California hybrids. Rios have had the most impact so far but more Merriam's are being brought in and it is hoped they'll range higher than Rios and make more use of national forest lands. In addition, a small flock of 36 eastern wild turkeys from Pennsylvania was released in southwestern Trinity County in 1993 and Rio/eastern hybrids from Kansas have since been introduced into San Diego, Trinity, Glenn, Mendocino and Alpine counties.

California seems to be a melting pot for gobblers as well as people. For that reason I won't be disappointed if my next tom doesn't match the description of any particular subspecies of wild turkey. Turkeys cross breed freely wherever the ranges of the various subspecies overlap and that means that some of the turkeys we hunt are hybrids.

In California the number of turkey hunters is increasing every year as are the opportunities to hunt. Ultimately, the over all population of turkeys, and the amount of habitat left unaltered by the works of man, as the state's human population continues to grow, will determine the amount of turkey hunting available in this state. For the time being, however, it's hard to predict what the end result will be but it's safe to assume that growth of the sport has not peaked by any means.

A few years ago I got some figures from the late Chuck Graves, then a wildlife biologist with the DFG, who was deeply involved in the wild turkey program here. Chuck guessed that there were probably

40,000 wild turkeys present in the state at that time. No one really knows how many wild turkeys there are roaming the woodlands of California today but it's safe to say that it's considerably more than 100,000.

When compared with some states east of the Mississippi there really isn't much hunting pressure yet on California turkeys. There is potential for considerable growth here and the more hunter interest there is the better it is for the turkey program. One of the brightest spots in the DFG game plan here recently is the introduction of Merriam's turkeys from South Dakota. The birds were released on public land in San Bernardino, Mendocino and Siskiyou counties and on a private ranch in

Oregon hunter Phil Vandergriff proves that turkey hunting can be good in his state, too.

Kern County where a limited amount of public hunting now takes place. Apparently more Merriam's are forthcoming and that's definitely good news.

The newcomer to the sport of wild turkey hunting has to start somewhere and the nearest regional office of the DFG is the logical first contact to make. The addresses are: Department of Fish and Game, Region 1, 601 Locust St., Redding, CA 96001 (916-225-2300); Region 2, 1701 Nimbus Rd., Rancho Cordova, CA 95670 (916-358-2900); Region 3, 7329 Silverado Trail, Box 47, Yountville, CA 94599 (707-944-5500); Region 4, 1234 East Shaw Ave., Fresno, CA 93710 (209-222-3761); Region 5, 330 Golden Shore, Suite 50, Long Beach, CA 90802 (310-590-5132).

Like most other western states **Oregon** boasts a growing population of wild turkeys and opportunities for hunting are increasing. In fact, for the first time the Beaver State was open to non-quota hunting during 1987 and no drawing has since been required. The limit now (1996) is two male turkeys except that an additional male turkey may be taken by hunters with a bonus tag for the southwestern region. Be sure to check the regulations for specifics.

Hunters have the Oregon Department of Fish and Wildlife, and the Rio Grande's capacity for reproduction to thank for this encouraging turn of events. Wild turkeys first came to Oregon in the 1950's when Merriam's turkeys were introduced on the east slope of the Cascade Range, where they never offered more than token sport for hunters.

Things started to change with the first introduction of Rio Grande turkeys in 1975. They prospered in the oak/madrone habitat found in Jackson County and more releases were made in similar habitat in other counties during ensuing years. In 1987, for instance, 200 Rios were imported from Texas and more recently the department of fish and wildlife has actively trapped and transplanted turkeys (up to 800 per year) from the state's own resident flocks.

Oregon has quite a bit of habitat suitable to turkeys and the best hunting currently is in the southwestern part of the state between Medford and Roseburg in Jackson, Lane and Douglas counties. Other prime counties are Josephine, Coos and Curry. Turkeys are found on the Umpqua National Forest near Tiller and Drew, on BLM land in the Applegate and Rogue River country and on both the Siskiyou and Rogue national forests. There are also turkeys on Mt. Hood National Forest lands and a few are taken each season on the eastern slope of Mt. Hood.

When I hunted in Oregon I learned two things. First, even a non-resident can locate and kill a tom there if he prospects for information in advance and then spends enough time scouting new country. I also found that some of the wet spring roads can be terrible.

Do your homework and try to determine, in advance, if a 4-WD vehicle will be needed during inclement weather, or if you can walk into the hunting area without one.

The best may be yet to come as far as Oregon turkey hunting is concerned. The introduction of Rio Grandes was a real eye opener and there's no reason to think they won't continue to expand their range in future years. For information and regulations contact the Oregon Department of Fish and Wildlife, P.O. Box 59, Portland, OR 97207 (503-229-5454).

When I contacted the **Washington** Department of Wildlife to talk about the wild turkey program a few years ago, I was told that the birds probably didn't have a bright future there and that the total population may have peaked at around 1,200 to 2,000 birds. Well, time again has a way of changing one's outlook and there are now more turkey hunters than that!

The difference, again, was the introduction of Rio Grande turkeys from both Oklahoma and Texas to parts of southcentral Washington, especially the Wenas area north of Ellensburg, starting in 1984.

"Despite a couple of severe winters we've seen excellent reproduction in those areas," said Dan Blatt, former upland game manager for the department, ""and we're looking forward to introducing Rios in several other locations. Generally, there's been a startling turn around from the dour predictions of the late 1970's and what Washington is experiencing may be symbolic of things taking place throughout the West. Dan Blatt said he thinks the best habitat may yet to be stocked. That's the oak belt country generally south of Yakima which is similar to terrain in Oregon where the turkeys are doing so well. The old mainstay for turkey hunting in Washington is Klickitat County in the southcentral region. Other counties with promise are Lincoln and Stevens in the southeast. Public lands include portions of the Umatilla National Forest and the Wootin, Asotin Creek and Chief Joseph wildlife areas.

While the actual take of turkeys is still small in Washington, about 500 per year, the future does look bright for hunters entering the sport there. Questionable weather has been a problem in the state but with more areas to choose from hunters may be able to adapt as the situation warrants.

As of 1996 hunters can take one bearded turkey from each subspecies in the state, Rio Grande, Merriam's and eastern wild turkeys. For information on spring and fall seasons contact the Washington Department of Wildlife, 600 Capitol Way N., Olympia, WA 98501 (360-902-2200).

Rob Hazelwood with a nice Montana Merriam's tom.

MOUNTAIN STATES

Some western mountain states always had some wild turkeys on the Merriam's variety and **Colorado** was one of them. Currently the Merriam's population stands at around 16,000 and the population trend has been up since disease problems occurred on the Uncompahgre Plateau in the mid-1980's.

The state division of wildlife is now conducting more trap and transplant operations, some of which are aimed at establishing Rio Grande populations in areas that may be better suited to them than native Merriam's. While there are turkeys in scattered locations from one side of the state to the other there are some areas with unlimited permits available and others where a drawing is held. The highest over all concentration of birds seems to be in Custer, Huerfano, Fremont, Costilla and Las Animas counties.

Except for some limited permit hunts, licenses are available over the counter in Colorado. Public areas in the southeast portion of the state include the Lake Dorothey and Spanish Peaks wildlife areas in the Trinidad region and the new John James Wildlife Area adjacent to Lake Dorothey. Other public hunting is found on the Uncompahgre and San Juan national forests.

The general spring season limit is one bearded turkey, however hunters who draw a limited entry permit can take a second bird. There is also a fall season. For information contact the Colorado Division of Wildlife, 6060 Broadway, Denver, CO 80216 (303-297-1192).

I really doubt if anyone knows how many wild turkeys the state of **Idaho** has right now. Apparently, for some hunters like my friend Ed Sweet, there are enough for some pretty good hunting. When I hunted with Ed a few years ago he showed me plenty of turkeys for an exciting, productive hunt. The annual harvest, just a few dozen birds a decade ago, has jumped to at least 1,500 turkeys today. Ninety percent of Idaho's wild turkeys are the Merriam's variety and roughly 10 percent are Rio Grandes.

Most of the turkeys are found along the west side of the state roughly from Boise north to the Canadian border. Generally speaking, finding a place to hunt on public land is no problem as there are turkeys on the Payette, Nez Perce and St. Joe national forests. Most hunting pressure occurs on the Payette National Forest because of its close proximity to population centers. To get away from some of the competition some hunters are now looking to areas north of the Salmon River.

Ultimately, the availability of mast during the winter may determine the future of Idaho's wild turkey population but for now the trend is definitely up and hunter interest is growing. The limit is one bearded or male turkey. Contact the Idaho Department of Fish and Game, 600 S. Walnut, P.O. Box 25, Boise, ID 83707 (208-334-3000).

In **Montana** interest in turkey hunting is continuing to grow as is the population of wild turkeys. The southeast portion has the most birds but approximately 75 percent of the 30,000 square mile region is private land where getting permission to trespass can be difficult. However, Neil Martin, a biologist with the state game department in Miles City, noted that there are turkeys on the Ashland and Sioux districts of the Custer National Forest where anyone can hunt. Special permits are not required for Hill, Chouteau, Fergus, Wheatland, Golden Valley, Yellowstone and Bighorn counties and all counties lying east of these. There are also special permit hunting areas in the western portion.

It's unusual, but Montana works only with Merriam's turkeys. For that reason the land of the Big Sky is an ideal place to go for a pure strain Merriam's wild turkey.

The limit in the spring is one wild, male turkey. A fall season is also held. For information contact the Montana Department of Fish, Wildlife and Parks, 1420 E. Sixth, Helena, MT 59620 (406-444-2535).

When I reported on wild turkeys in **Nevada** in the first edition of this book, there was no turkey hunting in the Silver State. My, how things have changed there. Today a limited number of resident and nonresident hunters can pursue Rio Grande turkeys on private lands in Lahonton and Paradise valleys (consult the regulations for the proper procedure) and on state lands such as the Mason Valley Wildlife Area and the Lahonton State Recreation Area.

Currently Nevada has approximately 2,000 Rio Grande turkeys and the birds are being introduced into still more areas. For information contact the Nevada Department of Wildlife, P.O. Box 10678, Reno, NV 89520 (702-688-1500).

As is the case practically everywhere in the West, interest in turkey hunting is growing in **Utah**. A small number of Merriam's turkeys is established in the state and Rio Grandes are being introduced into more and more places. Spring weather in Utah can cause access problems due to mud and snow and that can be discouraging. However, dedicated turkey hunters will find a way. Could be the best hunting will take place late in the spring season.

In 1996 there were 22 limited permit turkey hunts in Utah and plans to add more in the near future. The limit is one male turkey. For information contact the Utah Division of Wildlife Resources, 1596 W. North Temple, Salt Lake City, UT 84116 (801-538-4700).

Wyoming has a thriving population of Merriam's turkeys and some Rio Grandes have been introduced. The biggest population is in

John Higley is pleased with is fine Merriam's tom from Wyoming.

Crook and Weston counties but generally the northcentral and eastern parts of the state are well populated. Much of the good hunting land in the northeast section is on the Black Hills National Forest and is public. Unit 1, which is located there, is probably the best spot in the state.

In the spring of 1990 and 1991 I hunted the Black Hills near Newcastle with several companions and we all shot fine Wyoming toms on public land. Then we crossed the border into South Dakota and found willing gobblers there. That's one area I plan to visit again.

For the time being things have changed a bit in Unit 1. Formerly turkey permits were unlimited there but the turkey population was hit by harsh winter weather in 1992-93 and hunters are now required to get their tags in a drawing for all Wyoming turkey hunting. For application dates and other information contact the Wyoming Game and Fish Department, 5400 Bishop Blvd., Cheyenne, WY 82006 (307-777-4600).

This tom was taken by John Higley at 7,000 feet elevation in northeastern New Mexico.

SOUTHWEST

Arizona is one state that had wild turkeys historically and has also benefitted from modern management techniques in recent years. For instance, attempts have been made recently to replenish historic populations of Gould's turkeys in the mountains south of Tucson with turkeys that are already present on the Mexican side of the border.

Basically, Merriam's turkey range in Arizona extends from the town of Williams through the northcentral timber belt to the New Mexico border. Apparently, there's a thriving population in the north Kaibab region also. In addition to state regulated turkey hunting some Indian lands, like the Fort Apache and San Carlos reservations, also have birds and the tribes set their own fees, seasons and bag limits.

As is the case elsewhere on Merriam's turkey range, high elevation sometimes translates into foul (if not fowl) weather, especially during the early part of the spring season. Happily, public land is abundant and hunters have a good opportunity to find turkeys on the Apache Sitgreaves, Kaibab, Coconino, Prescott and Tonto national forests.

Permits for spring and fall hunts are issued by drawing well before the seasons come around. Get the information early by contacting the Arizona Game and Fish Department, 2222 W. Greenway RD., Phoenix, AZ 85023 (602-942-3000).

Because I've hunted there three times, **New Mexico** holds a special spot on my list of favorite turkey hunting places. There are Rio Grande turkeys in a couple of areas but mostly Merriam's are hunted here and I can vouch for the high population in the northeast corner of the state where I've hunted most.

The population of Merriam's turkeys, about 29,000 birds, is stable or increasing in most areas and there's good public access in the Sangre de Cristo, San Juan and Sacramento mountains on the Santa Fe, Lincoln, and Carson national forests. Rio Grandes are found in the Rio Grande Valley and along the Canadian and Mora rivers.

There are both spring and fall turkey seasons here and most permits are available over the counter. For information contact the New Mexico Department of Game and Fish, Villagra Building, Box 25112, Santa Fe, NM 87505 (505-827-7911).

Turkey hunting in the West can be very productive as this photo shows.

Chapter 15

Trophy And Meat Care

Turkeys and turkey hunting are special and it's natural for a hunter to want to keep some momento from each successful hunt. This can range from a beard in a drawer to a full body mount of a particularly memorable tom, perhaps your first or biggest. You can make a necklace out of spurs by hollowing the section of leg bone to which they're attached or you can remove the fan in its entirety and mount it open on a board. Some hunters take the whole skin of a turkey, feathers attached, of course, and tack it up on the wall or drape it over a counter.

If you decide you want to have a tom mounted there are some things to take into consideration. Sometimes, the birds flop violently after being shot and they can lose handfuls of feathers in the process, making it difficult, if not impossible, for a taxidermist to produce a decent looking mount later on. If I happen to be hunting with someone who intends to have his tom mounted I try to pounce on the bird before it can flop and grab it by the legs to hold it up. This is interesting if the tom has sharp spurs and more than once (I should have learned by now, I know) I've had a tom twist around in my gloved hand and rip the cloth, which could easily have happened to my hand, as well.

A tom would tend to spin even more if grabbed by the head, and if you tear at a wingtip you'll come away with a handful of primary feathers. In any event a good mount starts as soon as the tom drops and it's up to you not to let the feathers fly should the bird start flopping in the grass or kicking itself down a hill.

Next you have to transport the bird back to your camp or vehicle, and that usually means over your shoulder somehow. Obviously, the feathers will rub on you if you're not careful, and since it's inconvenient to hold a tom at arm's length for any amount of time, it should be wrapped up in something for the hike out. I haven't done it but I understand you can put a tom into a large nylon stocking head first,

This nice gobbler would qualify as a trophy in any man's book. He has a long beard and curved spurs.

so the feathers slide in easily, and remain in place. I've wrapped turkeys in small game bags to accomplish the same thing and there are turkey carrying tote sacks on the market these days that should work just fine. As I recall, they are hunter orange in color and well ventilated.

One of the longest beards I've seen was this one worn by a tom taken by Californian Al Tisserand. The beard measured 14-7/8 inches.

Contrary to popular belief you can sometimes have your turkey and eat it, too. If you're going to have it mounted, and can't take it to a taxidermist immediately, put the bird in your freezer whole. Don't even bother to field dress it. If it goes to the taxidermist promptly, say within a few days, he may actually be able to save most of the meat for you after skinning the bird and there shouldn't be anything wrong with it. Naturally, if you know how to skin a turkey for mounting you can do so while the bird is fresh but that's a skill that is best learned with the help of a taxidermist and it will take practice to master the operation.

Unfortunately, properly mounted, true to life turkeys, are few and far between. Most taxidermists simply don't get them right whether they position them standing, flying or in full strut. Mounting turkeys is an art in itself and it's much more involved than, say, ducks and geese of any kind. To get the body shape of turkeys just right one taxidermist I know has to build his own forms and even then he spends hours on the head (he doesn't like the comparatively new freeze dried or artificial head approach) and he has to work with every feather individually on a strutting tom mount. It's quite an operation, and he charges dearly for it, but his mounts are beautiful.

It seems that most taxidermists are better with one type of game than another, and that's understandable if they work on certain animals more than any others. Some are great on deer and elk, some do beautiful pronghorns or sheep, and a few specialize in fish or waterfowl. Very few have just the right touch for turkeys, and some simply don't want to be bothered because they feel they can't do a turkey right and make any money at all, which is also understandable.

So if you're particular, be sure to look at a taxidermist's work before you trust him with a tom and don't expect to pay the same price that you would for a goose because a turkey is much more difficult to do correctly.

The easiest trophy of all to keep is a tom's beard. You can twist it out or just cut it off at the breast, taking a little skin with it. Then put borax or salt on it until it dries. I put mine in the empty shotshell I use to collect the bird, and display it on a shelf with dozens more. There are all sorts of ways to display a collection of beards in your home or office.

Although your wife may not agree, a tail fan does make a nice wall ornament. I have one fan mounted on an oak plaque with the beard

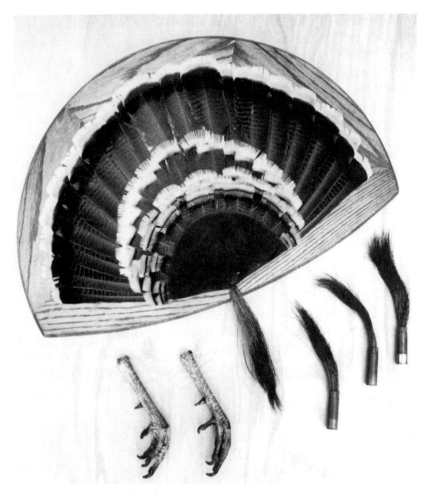

Some typical turkey trophies include the tail fan, beard(s) and feet. The fan and beard combination is mounted on an oak plaque.

hanging below it. A taxidermist did it for me but a handy hunter can do his own. There are tail fan mount kits available to make the job easier if you want to do it yourself. A framed photo of you with your trophy would look good beside the fan, as well.

I know some hunters with turkey legs displayed here or there, and while they are interesting to compare, others simply cut through the legs above and below the spurs with a bone saw or hacksaw and keep them instead. The tendon and bone marrow can then be removed easily. I can imagine the spurs on display with the beard or the spurs and beard on a plaque with a tail fan.

140

Of course, if you hunt turkeys successfully you should feel obligated to utilize the meat if at all possible, as you would any edible game. Wild turkeys have weaned more than one hunter away from plastic wrapped store bought turkey for good. I've never had a bad trophy tom, jake or hen, and I think wild birds are actually tastier than those raised domestically.

Typical of turkey hunting, however, there is more than one way to process your kill and render it edible. Personally, I like to dry pluck my birds soon after they're killed, meaning within a few hours on a normally cool spring or fall day. You can keep from ripping the skin by taking pinches of feathers, rather than a handful, as you remove them. I normally remove the tail fan, and wingtips to the first joint, rather than plucking them and gaining nothing to eat. The beard can easily be removed at this time, also.

Unless I can't get back home or to my camp within a few hours, I save the field dressing for the plucking session. That way I can save the heart, liver, neck (if it's not riddled with shot) and gizzard and keep them clean at the same time. In the spring the toms will have a fatty sponge-like substance in their crop which I like to remove while others leave it in place. This is actually fat that helps carry a tom over from the harshness of winter through the spring mating period when he won't be feeding regularly. The sponge is not apparent in the fall.

Some hunters short-cut all this and simply skin their turkey(s). In fact, the meat, sliced thin, seasoned, dredged in flour, and pan fried, is delicious. However, I prefer traditional roast turkey which can be used in several different ways after the first meal is a memory. We likehot turkey sandwiches, turkey and noodles with gravy, and one of our favorite game meals is wild turkey enchiladas that are sinfully thick with melted cheese, sour cream and mild chili sauce. In addition, the carcass may be boiled for soup stock.

If you travel for turkey hunting, and more and more hunters have found this easy to do these days, you'll find turkeys are easy to transport home by ground or air. If you drive you can obviously tote along an ice chest to hold the meat and plenty of ice to keep it cool. The main thing is to dress the bird promptly and not to keep it unfrozen for too many days. In other states I've asked to put my dressed turkey(s) in a restaurant or store freezer where I've been trading. Normally I've been accommodated.

If you fly it may be possible to hunt turkeys from a motel base camp with a rented vehicle. I prefer to camp out, as I did on an

Some hunters have learned how to skin their turkeys in the field as Wyoming outfitter Ron Dube is doing here. The skin can be used in many ways and the meat is still delicious.

Oregon hunt, but I drove there. When flying I either make arrangements for local help in advance or plan on staying in town and hunting from there. Regardless, bringing a turkey home by air is nothing like transporting part of a caribou or moose, which I've done on occasion.

You can pack your gear in an ice chest and use it for the meat on your flight home and take an extra duffle for the rest of your belongings or you can keep things simple. One way is to take a waterproof duffle and stuff a cold or frozen (never warm) turkey, double wrapped in plastic bags naturally, into it with clothes or a sleeping bag for insulation or simply do the same thing with a cardboard box. I like the duffle idea but most of the time I obtain a box at a local store and put my plastic wrapped turkey into it with a sleeping bag surrounding the carcass. Then I duct tape the box closed, using plenty of tape, and write my name and address on it with an indelible marker. I just check the box through as baggage and so far I haven't lost an ounce of meat on the way home. Notice I have not mentioned the use of dry ice, which usually isn't necessary on one day cross country flights, and which must be reported to the airlines in advance.

Really fine turkey taxidermy is expensive but a trophy tom like this one being air brushed by award winning California taxidermist Alan Jeffers will offer memories for a lifetime.

143

Wild turkeys are sharp breasted and sleek and cut a much thinner profile than a typical supermarket bird. However, there's still a lot of meat on an average tom and knowing how you acquired the bird makes you appreciate the meals it provides that much more. You'll know you've arrived as a turkey hunter when round breasted birds are the exception rather than the norm in your household.

Don't sell any turkey short. Even a jake like this young tom being displayed by a happy western hunter is a worthy trophy.

Chapter 16

Useful Contacts

There are many manufacturers of turkey calls and other gear relevant to the sport of turkey hunting including instruction tapes and videos. A few of them will be listed below and they may serve as useful contacts for someone just starting out or living in an area where sporting goods stores stock practically everything imaginable but turkey calls and paraphernalia.

As I said earlier the type or make of call you choose is ultimately a matter of personal choice. I've used many brands and they all work. Right now I have three Cedar Hill diaphragms in my turkey pack for immediate use and Perfection and Quaker Boy calls for back-up. Next season that order could very well change—again. As for hand operated calls I always have some sort of slate call handy but the first call out of the pack, usually, is my trusted M.L. Lynch cedar box, which I bought prior to the first spring season here in California. Obviously it's like an old friend by now and I hate to think that I might wear it out or lose it someday. Anyway, here are a few of the call makers I'm familiar with.

Ashby Turkey Calls, P.O. Box 65, Houston, MO 65483 (417-967-3787).

Butski's Game Calls, 453 79th Street, Niagara Falls, NY 14304 (716-283-3504).

Cedar Hill Game Call Co., Route 2, Box 236, Downsville, LA 71234 (318-982-5632).

Custom Turkey Calls, Inc., 2314 Pennsylvania Ave., Hagerstown, MD 21740 (301-733-0373).

Hunter's Specialties, Inc., 5285 Rockwell Drive Northeast, Cedar Rapids, IA 52402 (319-395-0321).

Ben Lee Calls, Box 27, Coffeeville, AL 36524 (717-536-3276).

Leonard Lee Rue Enterprises, RTD 1, Box 39, Great Valley, NY 14741 (716-945-4521).

Lohman MFG. Co., Inc., 4500 Doniphan Drive, Neosha, MO 64850 (417-451-4438).

M.L.Lynch Co., Box 377, Liberty, MS 39645 (601-657-4306).

Philip S. Olt Company, Inc., P.O. Box 550, Pekin, IL 61554 (309-348-3633).

Penn's Woods Products, Inc., 19 West Pittsburgh Street, Delmont, PA 15626 (412-468-8311).

Perfection Turkey Call, Inc., P.O. Box 164, Stephenson, VA 22656 (703-667-4608.

Pittman Game Calls, Route 1, Box 837, Sumrall, MS 39482 (601-758-4428).

Primos Wild Game Calls, Inc., P.O. Box 12785, Jackson, MS 39236 (601-366-1288).

Quaker Boy Game Calls, Inc., 6426 West Quaker Street, Orchard Parks, NY 14127 (716-662-3979).

Eddie Salter Calls, P.O. Box 872, Brewton, AL 36427 (205-867-9440).

Wilderness Sound Productions, 1105 Main, Springfield, OR 97477 (503-741-0263).

Some of these companies may be featured in various sportsman's catalogs like Cabela's, and Gander Mountain and many others. They make shopping at home easy for those with no source of calls down the street.

Game department addresses were included in the state by state rundown and it's obvious that in addition to regulations and so on, maps are essential, especially when visiting a new area for the first time. Some sources follow.

U.S.D.A. Forest Service maps are available for individual national forests and a small fee, usually $1.00 each, is charged. First request a list of national forests in the region you're interested in, then place the order.

Region 1 (Montana and northern Idaho), Federal Building, Missoula, MT 59807 (406-329-3316).

Region 2 (Colorado, part of Wyoming), 11177 W. 8th Avenue, P.O. Box 25127, Lakewood, CO 80225 (303-234-3711).

Region 3 (Arizona, New Mexico), Federal Building, 517 Gold Avenue S.W., Albuquerque, NM 87102 (505-766-2401).

Region 4 (Nevada, Utah, Southern Idaho, Western Wyoming), Federal Building, 324 25th Street, Ogden, UT 84401 (801-626-3201).

Region 5 (California), 630 Sansome Street, San Francisco, CA 94111 (415-556-4310).

Region 6 (Oregon, Washington), 319 S.W. Pine Street, P.O. Box 3623, Portland, OR 97208 (503-221-3625).

Bureau Of Land Management maps are also available and may apply to turkey hunting in some areas. There will be a fee charged so start by obtaining a price list and a free Index Map for the state you're interested in. Contact the Bureau of Land Management State Office as follows:

Arizona——2400 Valley Bank Center, Phoenix, AZ 85073 (602-261-3873).

California——Federal Building, Room E-2841, 2800 Cottage Way, Sacramento, CA 95825 (916-484-4676).

Colorado——Colorado State Bank Building, 1600 Broadway, Denver, CO 80202 (303-837-4325).

Idaho——398 Federal Building, 550 W. Fort Street, Boise, ID 83724 (208-384-1401)

Montana——222 N. 32nd.Street, P.O. Box 30157, Billings, MT 59107 (406-657-6462).

Nevada——Federal Building, 300 Booth Street, Room 3008, Reno, NV 89509 (702-784-5451).

New Mexico——South Federal Place, Santa Fe, NM 87501 (505-988-6217).

Oregon and Washington——729 N.E. Oregon Street, P.O. Box 2965, Portland, OR 97208 (503-231-6281).

Utah——University Club Building, 136 S. Temple, Salt Lake City, UT 84111 (801-524-5311).

Wyoming——2515 Warren Avenue, P.O. Box 1828, Cheyenne, WY 82001 (307-778-2326).

Topographic Maps are very helpful in locating turkeys in the first place and letting you know what the terrain is like in advance. You may be able to get them locally from a sporting goods store or you can order them from:

U.S. Geological Survey, Branch of Distribution, Federal Center, Denver, CO 80225 (303-234-3832).

Ask for a free Index Map of the state you're interested in, and a price list, then place your order.

– Chapter 17 –

Looking Back, Gazing Ahead

Looking back on my addiction to turkey hunting I realize, again, how the sport has changed my life. True, family and work still do come first but I remember dozens of days when I started turkey hunting long before daybreak and still put in a full day of labor afterward. Because I live close to turkey country I hunt often, perhaps too often, if the weary feeling I have all through the spring means anything. I certainly don't have any trouble sleeping during turkey season and a gallon of coffee doesn't effect me at all.

Some would say I'm a glutton for punishment. Not only do I hunt near home, I drive or fly across state lines for turkeys, too.

"You went where for a turkey?" a friend will ask, "you must be nuts."

"Maybe," I'll reply stifling a yawn, "but it sure was fun."

I suppose I'm afraid I'll miss something if I don't at least try for a turkey even when the weather is questionable or when I'd much rather keep my eyes closed and toss the alarm halfway to the moon. No way am I "into them" everytime out. No way will I pretend the hunting's easy. If it was simple I doubt if I'd be out there, shivering in the woods in the chill at 3 a.m. or climbing one last ridge in the heat of midday, hoping to find a lonely gobbler on the far side. Many mornings I've waited for the first rays of sunlight, listening intently for any turkey sound, and hearing nothing but small birds chirping and insects buzzing around my face. And yet, it always seems to be worth the trouble.

It's worth it just to watch the world come alive on a spring morning. It's worth it for the peace I feel just being there and it's worth it for the chance to observe other wildlife, like deer, black bears, gray squirrels, owls, hawks, coyotes and who knows what all up close when they don't know you're there. It's worth it just to share a laugh with a good friend, a son or a daughter, and it's worth it when your companion gets a bird and you don't, especially if it's their first turkey and you helped by calling or simply sitting back and being unselfish.

One of the most memorable hunts I ever had was with my son Mark in 1987. Mark had been too busy with postgraduate college studies to join me in turkey hunting, or anything else, for several years. It was a good feeling to be with him on a friend's ranch at long last on that warm April morning.

Before daybreak we heard gobbles just 100 yards away in a roost area I discovered a couple of seasons before. I had a shotgun but I really had no intention of using it so I put it aside, snuggled up to a mature manzanita bush, and told the birds where we were with a few quiet tree yelps. I'd like to say they rushed right in when the three toms flew down but they were quickly joined by noisy hens and we watched them walk over a little rise and out of sight together.

Author's son, Mark Higley, with the California tom he got in 1987.

That might have been it but we let the flock rest for a couple of hours while we looked elsewhere without success.Then we came back to try again. It was one of the best moves we ever made for the birds weren't far away and we started the toms gobbling with our first series of yelps from the ridge they disappeared over. I doubt if they were 75 yards away. Moving a bit closer we found a place to sit and soon we were yelping and clucking like members of the flock. Once in awhile I even scratched the leaves like a feeding bird, and while I don't know if it made any difference, the turkeys stayed around.We even caught a glimpse of one now and then through the brush that separated us from them.

Still, it was a stalemate until the toms began to fight amongst themselves. Then one adult bird separated from the others and hiked back toward the roost site while the rest of the group went farther down the hill. When we didn't think we'd be seen by any of them we got in behind the loner and I started yelping loudly. The tom's booming reply was enough to send us diving for the nearest cover. Mark sat in front of me and I sprawled out on the ground behind and called with a diaphragm. When that longbeard came around the corner he was only 18 yards away and I can still hear Mark's delighted, "All right!" when the tom tumbled at his shot.

You just never know how things will turn out in any hunting situation and the sweet moments of success like that are certainly worth the effort and the challenge of days when nothing seems to go right and you come home empty handed. Come to think about it, that's not always bad. A hunter who doesn't see anything in the sport but meat in the freezer or "horns" on the wall (or in this case a beard or feathered cape) never really gets to the heart of the matter. Every hunt can be a learning experience, and not just about turkeys. Every hunt should also be enjoyable simply because you are viewing nature from a hunter's unique perspective, as part of the whole scene, and not as an outside observer like a visitor at the zoo.

Game management is good conservation. The presence of wild turkeys in the West is ample proof of that. The immediate future looks bright in most states but ultimately there will be a cut-off in population expansion simply because of habitat limitations and habitat alteration, which is evident in some parts of California already. By then there could, and should, be more opportunities on the vast tracts of public land throughout the West and more hunters taking advantage of them.

What can we do to assure turkey hunting for ourselves, and our children's children? For one thing we can try to understand the biological requirements of the birds themselves. If flocks are to remain healthy and viable we must not attempt to introduce semi-domestic so called wild strain turkeys into new areas on our own. It's been proven time and again that it doesn't work and the local predators are probably fat enough already. As much as we like to watch them we should not encourage wild flocks to come into contact with domestic fowl where they could encounter poultry diseases which might spread through an entire population and at the very least reduce the reproductive capacity of the wild stock.

I don't think turkey hunting is an affair that lasts only a few weeks each year, or that it's something to exploit without putting anything back. Perhaps the best thing you can do is to keep learning about wild turkeys. Read everything you can. Try to understand more about the birds than just how to kill them efficiently. Waterfowl hunters have Ducks Unlimited to represent their interests and to develop wetlands projects to create more waterfowl and protect habitat for all sorts of indigenous wildlife.

Turkey hunters have an organization in their corner, too. They can establish local chapters of the National Wild Turkey Federation (NWTF) or join chapters already in place. Just belonging to this national organization opens the door to reams of information and even help on local projects. It also gives you a unified voice and, thus, some political clout with state wildlife agencies. Years ago, when the first chapter of the NWTF was started in California only 13 prospective members showed up. Within a few years literally hundreds of people attended annual meetings and Wild Turkey Days.

For information contact the National Wild Turkey Federation, Wild Turkey Center, Edgefield, SC 29824.

The future expansion of wild turkeys, and the survival of flocks already in place, depends largely on the hunters' attitude as a resource user. Obviously, hunting of any kind requires an abundance of wildlife and that abundance depends on the habitat available and the conservation ethic that brought many native species of game, turkeys included, back from the brink of extinction.

Sportsmen in general have been a fragmented group. We debate each other over regional differences and individual preferences, and too often overlook the outside threats to the "other guy" as long as they don't immediately effect our own baliwick. And while we pull and tug at each other anti-hunters are coming through the back door like never before. There are signs of unification, however, and it will take the strength of numbers and political power to preserve the hunting we have in the years to come. Right now the future of wild turkey hunting in the West seems bright. It's my prayer that it remains so for generations to come.

May every western turkey hunt end like this for you.

If you would like to order additional copies of
HUNTING WILD TURKEYS IN THE WEST
send a check or money order for $15.95 to:

John Higley
c/o Higley's High Country
P.O. Box 120
Palo Cedro, CA 96073

All books will be autographed.